Cross-Language Search and Summarization of Text and Speech (CLSSTS2020)

Marseille, France
11 – 16 May 2020

Editors:

Kathy McKeown
Douglas W. Oard

Elizabeth Boschee
Richard Schwartz

ISBN: 978-1-7138-1256-2

LREC 2020
Language Resources and Evaluation Conference
11–16 May 2020

**Cross-Language Search and Summarization of
Text and Speech
(CLSSTS2020)**

PROCEEDINGS

Editors: Kathy McKeown (Chair), Douglas W. Oard, Elizabeth
(Liz) Boschee, and Richard Schwartz.

Proceedings of the LREC 2020
Cross-Language Search and Summarization of
Text and Speech
(CLSSTS2020)

Edited by: Kathy McKeown (Chair), Douglas W. Oard, Elizabeth (Liz) Boschee, and Richard Schwartz.

For more information:
European Language Resources Association (ELRA)
9 rue des Cordelières
75013, Paris
France
http://www.elra.info
Email: lrec@elda.org

Introduction

In today's global world, people may need access to information that only appears online in a language they do not speak. Cross-Language Information Retrieval (CLIR) enables end users to issue queries in their own language, but provides results from multiple languages around the world, often using translation so that the end user can quickly understand whether the retrieved results are relevant. Cross-language summarization can make it easier for an end user to determine if a document is relevant by providing a summary in the user's language of the foreign language document, highlighting the evidence for relevance. Alternatively, a summary can be used to get a sense of document meaning, when the document is not in the user's language. When the foreign language is a low-resource language, cross-language search and summarization are more difficult; translation capabilities may be poor and the lack of resources makes it difficult to train CLIR and summarization systems. To complicate matters even more, when the collection contains speech as well as text, producing accurate search results and generating comprehensible summaries is even more difficult.

This workshop aims to stimulate the collection and provision of resources that can improve systems that perform cross-language search and summarization. Papers were solicited that describe recent and current research in these areas, that describe relevant resources, or that stake out positions on the directions in which the authors think the field should move.

Had the workshop proceeded in person, it would have featured a keynote speech by Carl Rubino, program manager of the IARPA MATERIAL program (USA). Carl was planning to describe the program and the languages studied, as well as metrics that the program uses during its evaluations, paying particular attention to the correlation between linguistic properties and system performance. We had also planned a second keynote speech by Julio Gonzalo, Universidad Nacional de Educación a Distancia (Madrid, Spain), who has recently been working on reputation reports, summaries of what is being said about an entity with a focus on reputational consequences. They have collected a large multilingual test collection for the reputation monitoring problem, with over half a million manual annotations for several tasks on twitter data, including named-entity disambiguation, reputational polarity, topic detection, reputational alerts, reputation reports, opinion maker identification, reputational dimensions, and author profiling.

To set the stage, the organizers provide two small spoken language test collections that include waveforms, transcriptions and possibly queries with relevance judgments. These are conversational genres, one in Somali (a very-low resource language) and the other in Bulgarian (a moderate-resource language) both of which include approximately 80 hours of speech.

Organizing Committee

Kathy McKeown, Columbia University (USA), Chair
James Allan, University of Massachusetts at Amherst (USA)
Lu Wang, Northeastern University (USA)
Douglas W. Oard, University of Maryland (USA)
Steve Renals, University of Edinburgh (UK)
Elizabeth (Liz) Boschee, USC/Information Sciences Institute (USA)
Richard Schwartz, Raytheon BBN Technologies (USA), Editor

Program Committee

Eneko Agirre, University of the Basque Country (Spain)
Piyush Arora, American Express Big Data Labs (India)
Mohit Bansal, University of North Carolina (USA)
Nicola Ferro, University of Padua (Italy)
Petra Galuscakova, University of Maryland (USA)
Jan Hajic, Charles University (Czech Republic)
Gareth Jones, Dublin City University (Ireland)
Damianos Karakos, Reytheon BBN Technologies, (USA)
Jonathan May, University of Southern California Information Sciences Institute (USA)
Jessica Ouyang, University of Texas at Dallas (USA)
Pavel Pecina, Charles University (Czech Republic)
Kay Peterson, NIST (USA)
Dragomir Radev, Yale University (USA)
Hussein Suleman, University of Cape Town (South Africa)
Audrey Tong, NIST (USA)
Xabier Saralegi Urizar, Elhuyar Foundation (Spain)
Ilya Zavorin, Bluemont Technology (USA)
Rui Zhang, Yale University (USA)

Table of Contents

Proceedings of the Cross-Language Search and Summarization of Text and Speech Workshop, pages 1–6
Language Resources and Evaluation Conference (LREC 2020), Marseille, 11–16 May 2020

The Effect of Linguistic Parameters in Cross-Language Information Retrieval Performance
Evidence from IARPA's MATERIAL Program

Carl Rubino
Intelligence Advanced Research Projects Activity (IARPA)
Washington, DC 20511 USA
Carl.Rubino@iarpa.gov

Abstract
In IARPA's MATERIAL program, choosing languages and acquiring corpora to develop an effective End-to-End Cross-Language Information Retrieval (CLIR) system for speech and text, and component technologies thereof, was strategically planned to enable language-independent methods for CLIR development and evaluation. It was believed that a typologically diverse set of languages, coupled with a heterogeneous evaluation condition would stimulate participating research teams to construct engines that would be usable in diverse environments and responsive to changing data conditions. This paper will detail how the MATERIAL program investigated certain linguistic parameters to guide the language choice, data collection and partitioning, and better understand evaluation results.

Keywords: linguistic evaluation, cross-language information retrieval, linguistic parameters, language typology, NLP program design

1. Introduction

IARPA's Machine Translation for English Retrieval of Information in Any Language (MATERIAL) program was launched in 2017 to stimulate research on a wide array of human language technologies optimized to support cross-language information retrieval and summarization. Four multinational teams (led by Columbia University, Johns Hopkins University, Raytheon BBN and USC-ISI), chosen via competitive selection, were tasked to build End-to-End CLIR systems capable of retrieving in a fully automated way, foreign language speech and text documents responsive to a new typology of English queries, and provide evidence or relevance, in English, of the retrieved documents for human consumption (Rubino, 2017).

Prior to the 2017 kickoff of the program, nearly two years were devoted to negotiating the data collection, guided by the program's strategic evaluation methodology. This included separate training and testing conditions for both speech and text, a diverse set of languages to explore, and challenging development time frames that decreased as the program progressed.

IARPA collaborated with its Test and Evaluation (T&E) partners at the University of Maryland's Center for Advanced Study of Language (CASL), NSA's Center for Applied Machine Translation (CAMT), and MIT-Lincoln Laboratories to choose an optimal mix of diverse languages which would be incrementally released to the performing teams to stimulate and measure progress across three program periods. Two factors were most critical in initially determining the language choice: typological diversity, measured by divergent phonological, morphological and syntactic properties, and resource availability. To allow for the program's mismatch between the training and testing conditions and the requirement to identify domains without additional source language training, the languages eventually

collected and annotated also had to have a substantial presence on the web. This would enable the performing teams to harvest relevant data to complement the small training sets provided by IARPA to seed the CLIR system development. Web harvesting was crucial to the program to improve the performance of applications against genres not represented in the training data, e.g. for speech, all the training data were conversational telephony, but the evaluation condition included broadcast news (Rubino, 2019). IARPA followed a strict language release schedule, not divulging the language identities until the start of each relevant development phase. This ensured that progress could be measured temporally and consistently between teams. As of May 2020, six languages were provided. Listed in order of release, these were: Tagalog (TGL), Swahili (SWA), Somali (SOM), Bulgarian (BUL), Lithuanian (LIT) and Pashto (PUS).

2. The Metrics

It was important to IARPA to evaluate the systems on a meaningful task-based measure. The primary performance measure used to assess the CLIR aspect of performer systems was a novel detection metric, related to the keyword spotting metric Actual Term Weight Value ($ATWV$) used in the IARPA Babel program (Fiscus et al., 2007). The MATERIAL metric, Actual Query Weighted Value ($AQWV$), expresses an average of all Query Values for a system operating under its actual decision threshold. This allowed for all queries to be equally treated regardless of the number of documents annotated as relevant to them in the ground truth. Query Value (QV) is defined as:

$$QV = 1 - P_{Miss} - \beta \times P_{FA} \qquad (1)$$

where P_{Miss} is the probability that a relevant document for the query will not be detected (a miss against the ground truth), and P_{FA} is the probability that a non-relevant document will be incorrectly detected (a false alarm against the ground truth). The parameter β allowed for the relative weighting of misses and false alarms. It was derived from the following formula:

$$\beta = \frac{C}{V} \times \left(\frac{1}{P_{Rel}} - 1 \right) \tag{2}$$

where C is the cost of an incorrect detection, V is the value of a correct detection, and P_{Rel} is the prior probability that a document is relevant to the query. This value changed under different conditions but will remain constant for all data described herein. A perfect system that returned all relevant documents without false alarms would receive a score of 1. A system that did not return anything would receive a score of 0. If all the documents a system detected were false alarms, the score would be $-\beta$.

IARPA also provided roughly six hundred translated and transcribed documents, released as an Analysis Set, to allow the teams to measure component progress in speech recognition and machine translation (MT) using traditional metrics Word Error Rate (WER) and BLEU, respectively.

3. Linguistic Parameters Measured

Building CLIR systems capable of addressing both speech and text entails creating multiple component technologies, then learning how to optimally integrate them for information retrieval. Since a primary purpose of the MATERIAL program was to inspire novel research in both speech and translation, presumed challenges stemming from linguistic complexities and language anomalies were actively sought out by the T&E team as a means to advance research appropriately.

From a linguistic perspective, a number of parameters that could potentially affect system performance may immediately come to mind, to include both typological features of the languages such as phonetic inventory, morphological complexity, and word order, to sociolinguistic features to include dialectology, script standardization, literacy and diglossia. MATERIAL's T&E Team collected linguistic statistics on the candidate languages, focusing on features that were assumed to have a higher chance of correlation with Natural Language Processing (NLP) performance. For a sample of these kinds of linguistic variables, selected parameter values from the World Atlas of Language Structures (WALS) for the MATERIAL languages released so far are given in Table 1 with their numeric WALS Feature value (Dryer and Haspelmath, 2013). Parameters considered to be more challenging for NLP applications in the table are shown in bold.

For some linguistic features, typological resources do exist that enable us to quantify differences between or across languages. The URIEL knowledge base and its lang2vec utility, for example, provide vector identifications of languages measured from a variety of parameters taken from typological, geographical and phylogenetic databases to aid in NLP correlational analysis (Littell et al., 2017). Using lang2vec, vectors representing multiple syntactic features (often binary), manually drawn from WALS, and

the Syntactic Structures of the World Languages (Collins and Kayne, 2011) can be compared across languages to compute a relative distance between any set of languages for an available amalgamation of categories. While such vector values may appear to be helpful in differentiating languages by their features, some caveats should be noted. First, no weighting mechanism is introduced to calculate the vector; all categories, regardless of their potential effect on NLP applications are treated equally. Furthermore, not all languages in the collection are represented equally for all the typological dimensions measured. Some features, in fact, were predicted from typological inference and genetic relationships. Nevertheless, we felt a conglomerate distance measure derived from a wide variety of linguistic categories was worth investigating. Table 2 exemplifies the lang2vec tool's distance calculations between English and the MATERIAL languages for four dimensions: phonological features, syntactic features, a compound value of the product of phonological and syntactic distance, and phonetic inventory.

Because Automatic Speech Recognition (ASR) was an integral part of the program, the T&E Team paid considerable attention to phonological features and phonetic inventories of the languages they chose to roll out. Multiple resources were available to capture phonetic and phonological properties, then relay them to the performing teams with each language via a document entitled "Language Specific Design Document", jointly authored by CASL and the data collector Appen Butler Hill. To contrast the specific MATERIAL languages for this paper, we counted three inventories as shown in Table 3: the number of consonants, number of vowels, and the number of segments (composed of the number of consonants, vowels and tones). These measures were extracted from the Phoible database which provides online search through an intuitive interface (Moran and McCloy, 2019). Because no single database provides complete coverage of the languages for which phonetic inventories have been documented, Phoible contains multiple databases that often conflict with each other in their counts. Where differing counts in the Phoible database were encountered, the values cited in the UCLA Phonological Segment Inventory Database took precedence, followed by the Stanford Phonology Archive.

4. The Baseline Systems

To relate the linguistic features to current program progress, we will introduce results for several baseline systems contributing to the CLIR pipeline, as well as the CLIR system itself. These rudimentary systems were produced with minimal training data, often just the program build pack and other noted, publicly available low-hanging-fruit resources. Development for the program parameters was also minimal. Table 4 reports the component technology baselines in terms of BLEU (for machine translation) and WER (for speech recognition) calculated for the MATE-RIAL Analysis Set. For machine translation the following baselines were reported: a phrase based statistical (PBMT) system trained on the MATERIAL Build Pack augmented

WALS Feature, #	Tagalog	Swahili	Somali	Lithuanian	Bulgarian	Pashto
Consonants, 1A	Mod Small	Mod Large	Avg	**Large**	Avg	Mod Large
Vowel Quality, 2A	Avg (5-6)	Avg (5-6)	**Large** (7-14)	Avg (5-6)	Avg (5-6)	Avg (5-6)
Syllable Structure, 12A	Mod Complex	Simple	Mod Complex	**Complex**	**Complex**	**Complex**
Uncommon Consonants, 19A	None	*th* sounds	**Pharyngeals**	None	None	None
Case, 49A	None	None	3	6-7	No	3
Word Order, 81A	VSO	SVO	SOV	SVO	SVO	SOV

Table 1: WALS Parameters for the MATERIAL languages released so far.

Language	Distance Calculations from English			
	Phon.	Syn.	Phon * Syn	Inventory
TGL	0.3433	0.66	0.226578	0.461
SWA	0.2736	0.71	0.194256	0.484
SOM	0.4816	0.62	0.298592	0.465
LIT	0.3498	0.68	0.237864	0.469
BUL	0.2804	0.48	0.134592	0.521
PUS	0.5687	0.57	0.324159	0.598

Table 2: Lang2Vec values for chosen linguistic attributes (phonological, syntactic).

Lang.	Segments	Consonants	Vowels	Syllable Structure
TGL	23	18	5	Moderately Complex
SWA	36	31	5	Simple
SOM	32	22	10	Moderately Complex
LIT	52	36	16	Complex
BUL	42	36	6	Complex
PUS	38	31	7	Complex

Table 3: Phonetic Inventories from Phoible.

with the Long Now Foundation's PanLex lexicon available at panlex.org, and three neural MT (NMT) systems trained on the MATERIAL Build Pack with PanLex (NMT), with additional engines trained on additional in-language data available from a web harvest (NMT-Mono), and a third NMT engine that also includes training data from additional, often related, languages (NMT-Multi).

Model	TGL	SWA	SOM	LIT	BUL	PUS
	MT Baselines (BLEU)					
PBMT	33.0	22.8	17.3	17.6	32.3	13.3
NMT	27.9	23.6	14.7	19.5	33.3	N/A
NMT-Mono	N/A	N/A	N/A	29.8	43.1	12.6
NMT-Multi	38.7	35.4	22.3	30.2	43.2	17.5
	Speech Recognition Baselines (WER)					
CNN-LSTM	46.6	44.3	60.6	47.9	40.0	42.8
CNN-LSTM+	33.9	33.7	49.4	23.4	21.3	39.9

Table 4: MT and ASR Baselines.

The ASR baselines reported involve a CNN Long Short-Term Memory Network (CNN-LSTM) system trained on MATERIAL Audio Build data and 1500 hours from several languages, including languages released in the Babel program, English and Arabic. The CNN-LSTM+ model cited also includes an expanded model and lexicon generated from a web text harvest and lexicon which significantly decreased the Out-of-Vocabulary (OOV) rate and improved WER scores.

The CLIR baselines detailed in Table 5 reflect the AQWV results from the MATERIAL Analysis Set, with separate numbers provided for retrieval on text vs. speech, presented as Text / Speech. For the first three languages of the program, Tagalog, Swahili and Somali, the low resource conditions were augmented with a web harvest that include Panlex and data from DARPA's LORELEI program. These additional resources were incrementally included in the CLIR systems for Lithuanian, Bulgarian, and were not present in Pashto.

5. Correlates of Performance

Because ASR systems for the MATERIAL languages were trained with multilingual features without regard to English, we initially only investigated what we considered to be potential correlations between the syntactic vectors with two program tasks that would require English language transfer: machine translation (via BLEU) and CLIR (via AQWV). We found no strong correlation between the English syntactic distance vectors and the MT task measured by BLEU (NMT $r(4) = -.09$, PBMT $r(4) = -.22$), see Figure 1, or the CLIR Task measured by AQWV (Text $r(4) = .03$, Speech $r(4) = .20$). A number of reasons can be postulated for why no correlation would exist between CLIR scores and English distance scores, such as highly diverse datasets measured for information retrieval per language, non-uniform averaged relevance probabilities for the query sets built for each language, and varying degrees of complexity between the query sets used to evaluate each language. While the number of queries released per language was relatively uniform, the composition of query types was not. More detailed descriptions of the query typology and datasets can be found in the MATERIAL Evaluation plan here: https://bit.ly/39cNGoo.

Surprisingly, when we compared MT performance to phonological distance, we found a strong negative correlation with NMT BLEU $r(4) = -.93$, $p = .008$; but not

Model	Tagalog	Swahili	Somali	Lithuanian	Bulgarian	Pashto
Baseline	-	-	-	32.0 / 14.5	41.3 / 19.4	47.3 / 38.7
+Paracrawl	-	-	-	60.5 / 22.9	64.6 / 29.9	-
+Paracrawl+Web	59.4 / 57.9	44.8 / 33.0	22.6 / 9.9	66.3 / 63.3	72.9 / 68.8	-

Table 5: CLIR Baselines in terms of AQWV (Text/Speech).

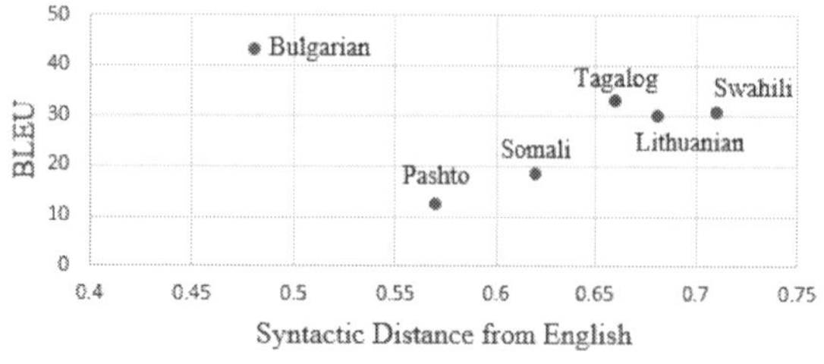

Figure 1: Syntactic Distance from English vs. BLEU

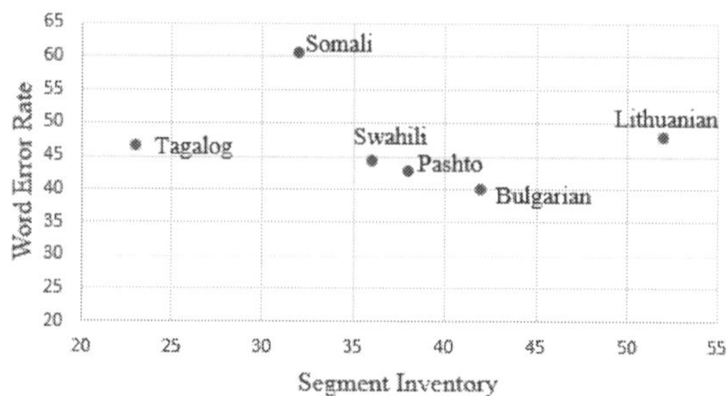

Figure 3: Segment Inventory vs. CNN-LSTM WER.

against PBMT performance where $r(4) = -.72, p = .106$. To compare MT performance with a more intuitive measure, we calculated a new compound linguistic measure, the product of syntactic and phonological distance, where the negative correlation with NMT and PBMT is more apparent and significant, $r(4) = -.95, p = .004$. See Table 2.

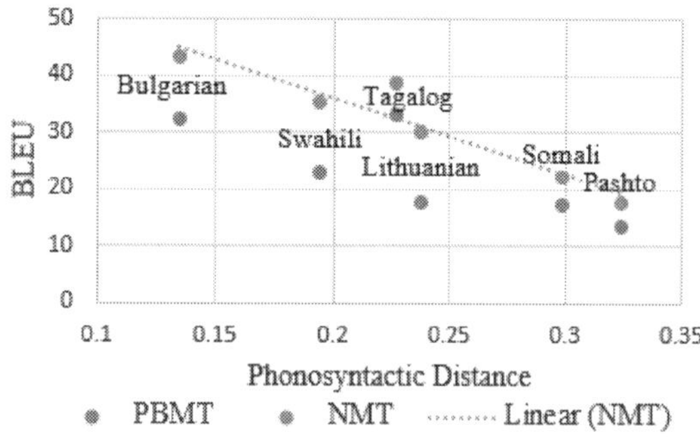

Figure 2: Phono-syntactic distance with NMT BLEU.

Not surprisingly, exploring the segment counts detailed in Table 3 to compare with a baseline CNN-LSTM monolingually trained engine yielded no evidence of correlation, $r(4) - .24, p = .642$ (Figure 3). Even less surprising was the observation that the Inventory Distance vector from English and ASR performance on the CNN-LSTM system were also not correlated, $r(4) = -.53, p = .281$. Much diversity was present in the program's speech data. The audio used for evaluation was somewhat consistent for genre distribution and sampling rates between languages but not for recording quality, or other critical factors such as the amount of data with music, dialect diversity in the collection or the number of speakers recorded.

Categorizing languages with absolute features can be intriguing theoretically, but most advantageous to the performers and the T&E team were quantifiable measures derived from program corpora. One way, for instance, of projecting possible lexical coverage problems would be to calculate OOV rates existing between development and test partitions of the IARPA released training data. Languages with higher OOV rates may presumably have lexical gaps in text and possibly, transcription anomalies in speech. Table 6 shows OOV counts calculated from the BBN team, to include both IARPA-provided corpora and their harvest.

Lang.	Text			Speech	
	Parallel training (words)	% OOV		ASR Training (hours)	% OOV
TGL	1,950k	4.3		128	5.5
SWA	1,738k	5.0		68	12.7
SOM	2,278k	13.7		48	18.0
LIT	18,939k	3.7		66	2.6
BUL	25,984k	1.5		41	1.4

Table 6: OOV rates calculated by training partition.

The text OOV rates did indeed correlate with the performance of the NMT engine trained with multilingual data, perhaps as a function of the effectiveness of each language's data harvest of differing sizes to lower the OOV rates, $r(3) = -.87, p = .005$. Likewise, the LSTM+ ASR engine performance correlates to the OOV rates observed in speech, $r(3) = .93, p = .022$. See Figures 4 and 5.

For seeding machine translation development, IARPA provided training data for each language consisting of sentence-aligned bitexts from multiple news sources. To maximize diversity of the rather homogeneous collection, no more than five sentences were taken from the same article. Table 7 provides the word counts for these training corpora, along with translation ratios (foreign

Language	# Words	# Unique Words	# Translated Words	# Unique Translated Words	Unique Word Ratio	Translation Ratio
SWA	718562	55814	807766	31455	0.07767	0.88957
TGL	782525	50903	809547	30114	0.06505	0.96662
SOM	734132	73941	758337	21935	0.10072	0.96808
BUL	723042	71404	817910	35025	0.09875	0.88401
LIT	607274	91809	834541	30821	0.15118	0.72767
PUS	975595	59815	809597	28026	0.06131	1.20504

Table 7: MATERIAL MT Training Data Statistics.

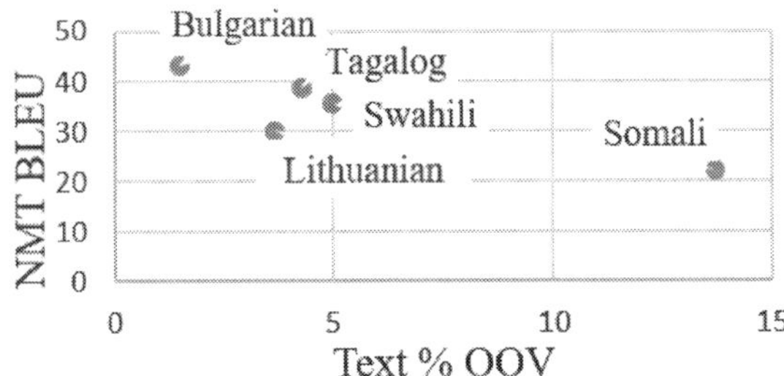

Figure 4: ASR performance as correlated to text OOV.

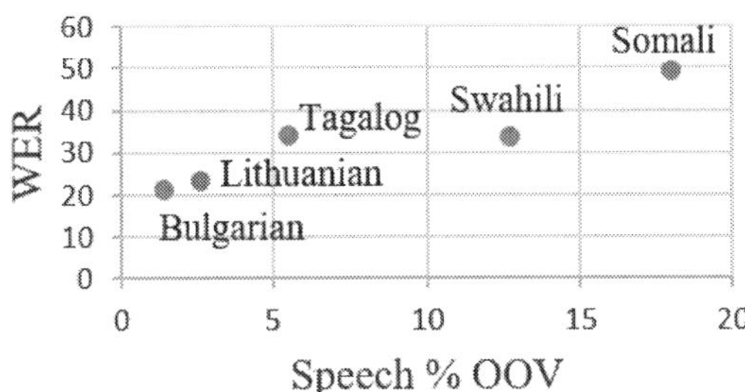

Figure 5: ASR performance as correlated to speech OOV.

Lang.	Vocabulary size at 80K words (K words)	OOV(%) with Acoustic Build Data
TGL	11.3	13.5
SWA	13.1	14.1
SOM	12.2	15.7
BUL	13.1	13.3
LIT	19.4	21.3
PUS	7.2	6.0

Table 8: Vocabulary statistics from the Speech Build packs.

6. Conclusion

From the IARPA MATERIAL experience, choosing languages by linguistic parameters helps to ensure parametric diversity, critical to our ability to develop language-independent CLIR solutions in low resource conditions, a fundamental question posed by the program. Certain typological parameters we may assume to be tightly linked to CLIR results often have no correlation with the actual performance of the NLP applications to which the parameters would seem intuitively relevant. Discerning which linguistic parameters correlated with overall performance enabled IARPA to evaluate CLIR progress when different languages were measured. Some parameters were also a significant factor for Performing Teams to determine the most effective CLIR pipeline design, customized to handle language-specific properties deemed necessary to address. These pipelines, as well as data collection and use strategies, differed between teams and languages, the details of which are beyond the scope of this paper.

We have shown, albeit with a relatively small sample of diverse languages and only using immature baseline systems, that amalgamate typological distance vectors between the MATERIAL languages and English quite unexpectedly and counter-intuitively did correlate with MT BLEU scores, but not AQWV or WER measures.

We suggest that when choosing languages to design or evaluate an NLP research program, ample attention is paid to the language dimension as measured by the properties of the data used for both training, development and evaluation, as their correlation with performance is likely to exceed that of typological parameters presumed to be critical from a linguistic perspective.

words/English words) and unique word ratios (unique source words/all source words). We investigated the unique word ratio as a potential correlate for vocabulary growth. Higher ratios indicating larger vocabulary expansion may derive from a variety of factors, such as lack of orthographic standards, segmentation anomalies, or increased morphological complexity. There was a weak negative correlation between the NMT Multilingual BLEU result and the unique word ratio, $r(4) = .73, p = .101$.

Comparing baseline BLEU scores against the unique word ratios at the bitext size of 800K foreign language words offered slight evidence of correlation for NMT $r(4) = -.73, p = .101$ but not for PBMT performance, BLEU $r(4) = -.48, p = .339$. Likewise, no correlation was found between BLEU scores and vocabulary size in a smaller speech dataset of 80K words shown in Table 8, PBMT $r(4) = .06, t = .911$, NMT $r(4) = .36, t = .489$.

7. Acknowledgments

Special thanks to Timothy McKinnon for introducing me to lang2vec and fruitful discussions on linguistics and evaluation. I am also grateful to Audrey Tong, Catherine Cotell, and the anonymous editors of this volume for their comments on a previous version of this paper. This work is supported by the Office of the Director of National Intelligence (ODNI), Intelligence Advanced Research Projects Activity (IARPA). The views and conclusions contained herein are those of the author and should not be interpreted as necessarily representing the official policies, either expressed or implied, of ODNI, IARPA, or the U.S. Government. The U.S. Government is authorized to reproduce and distribute reprints for governmental purposes notwithstanding any copyright annotation therein.

8. Bibliographical References

Collins, C. and Kayne, R. (2011). *Syntactic Structures of the World's Languages*. New York University, New York.

Dryer, M. and Haspelmath, M. (2013). *The World Atlas of Language Structures Online*. Leipzig, Germany: Max Planck Institute for Evolutionary Anthropology.

Fiscus, J. G., Ajot, J., Garofolo, J. S., and Doddingtion, G. (2007). Results of the 2006 spoken term detection evaluation. In *Proceedings of the ACM SIGIR Workshop on Searching Spontaneous Conversational Speech*, pages 51–55. ACM SIGIR.

Littell, P., Mortensen, D. R., Lin, K., Kairis, K., Turner, C., and Levin, L. (2017). Uriel and lang2vec: Representing languages as typological, geographical, and phylogenetic vectors. In *Proceedings of the 15th Conference of the European Chapter of the Association for Computational Linguistics: Volume 2, Short Papers*, pages 8–14.

Steven Moran et al., editors. (2019). *PHOIBLE 2.0*. Jena: Max Planck Institute for the Science of Human History.

Rubino, C. (2017). *MATERIAL Broad Agency Announcement*. https://bit.ly/37gKhV9.

Rubino, C. (2019). IARPA's Contribution to Human Language Technology Development for Low Resource Languages. In *Language Technologies for All Conference*. UNESCO. https://bit.ly/39e2mD4.

Corpora for Cross-Language Information Retrieval in Six Less-Resourced Languages

Ilya Zavorin, Aric Bills, Cassian Corey, Michelle Morrison, Audrey Tong, Richard Tong

Bluemont Technology and Research Inc, UMD Applied Research Laboratory for Intelligence and Security (ARLIS),
MIT Lincoln Lab, UMD ARLIS, National Institute of Standards and Technology, Tarragon Consulting Corporation
Luray, VA, USA, College Park, MD, USA, Lexington, MA, USA, College Park, MD, USA, Gaithersburg, MD, USA,
Berkeley, CA, USA

ilya.zavorin@bluemonttechnology.com, abills@umd.edu, cassian.corey@ll.mit.edu, mmorriso@umd.edu,
audrey.tong@nist.gov, rtong@tgncorp.com

Abstract

The Machine Translation for English Retrieval of Information in Any Language (MATERIAL) research program, sponsored by the Intelligence Advanced Research Projects Activity (IARPA), focuses on rapid development of end-to-end systems capable of retrieving foreign language speech and text documents relevant to different types of English queries that may be further restricted by domain. Those systems also provide evidence of relevance of the retrieved content in the form of English summaries. The program focuses on Less-Resourced Languages and provides its performer teams very limited amounts of annotated training data. This paper describes the corpora that were created for system development and evaluation for the six languages released by the program to date: Tagalog, Swahili, Somali, Lithuanian, Bulgarian and Pashto. The corpora include build packs to train Machine Translation and Automatic Speech Recognition systems; document sets in three text and three speech genres annotated for domain and partitioned for analysis, development and evaluation; and queries of several types together with corresponding binary relevance judgments against the entire set of documents. The paper also describes a detection metric called Actual Query Weighted Value developed by the program to evaluate end-to-end system performance.

Keywords: Cross-Language Information Retrieval, Less-Resourced Languages, Queries, Speech, Text

1. Introduction

In recent years, deep learning methods revolutionized many areas of Natural Language Processing (NLP) research, including Cross-Language Information Retrieval (CLIR) and Cross-Language Summarization (CLS). CLIR allows users to retrieve relevant content in one or more languages different from the language of the user's query, while CLS provides a way for the user to assess relevance of retrieved foreign-language documents without knowing the language of those documents. While such capabilities are critical to allow monolingual speakers access to foreign data, the amount of training data of sufficient quality often required by deep learning based methods to perform well is simply not available for many less-resourced languages of the world. Even though the amount of digital content the world produces increases tremendously every year, the situation is further complicated by the need to rapidly adapt NLP technologies to new languages, genres and domains.

First conceived in 2015 and launched by the Intelligence Advanced Research Projects Activity (IARPA) in 2017, the Machine Translation for English Retrieval of Information in Any Language (MATERIAL) research program research program is designed to address these challenges (Rubino, 2017). MATERIAL grew out of the Babel program (Harper, 2011) which focused on rapid development of methods to support robust keyword search of large collections of noisy conversational speech. Like Babel, MATERIAL focuses on rapid development of systems for Less-Resourced Languages (LRLs) using limited resources, but it aims at propelling research in a wider array of technologies. MATERIAL performers are tasked with building End-to-End or English-in/English-out (E2E) systems capable of retrieving foreign language speech and text documents relevant to different types of English queries that may be restricted by domain, and providing evidence of relevance of the retrieved documents to both the query string and domain. This evidence is presented in the form of English query-biased summaries.

This paper describes several corpora that were developed for each MATERIAL language. These include (i) annotated Machine Translation (MT) and Automatic Speech Recognition (ASR) build packs, (ii) document sets in three text and three speech genres annotated for domain and partitioned for analysis, development and evaluation, and (iii) queries of several types together with corresponding binary relevance judgments against the entire set of documents. These full-annotation corpora enable exploration of both high-precision and high-recall retrieval of a diverse set of LRLs, unlike more classical IR evaluations such as TREC (Voorhees and Harman, 2005) or CLEF (Ferro and Peters, 2019) that have historically focused on high-resource languages and/or relied on post-hoc annotation.

MATERIAL E2E systems would require high-quality component technologies such as MT and ASR. However, scoring high on standard component quality metrics such as BLEU or WER does not guarantee commensurate performance on downstream tasks (such as retrieval). Therefore, MATERIAL introduced a novel E2E evaluation protocol that combines automatic and human evaluation. While the details of this protocol are beyond the scope of this paper, we present here its central component, which is a detection metric called Actual Query Weighted Value (AQWV) designed to measure quality of both retrieval and summarization.

2. MATERIAL Languages

Table 1 lists MATERIAL LRLs released to date. These languages were selected to create a broad evaluation portfolio consisting of languages with significant Internet presence from different language families to provide diverse phonotactic, morphological, and syntactic characteristics. To encourage rapid system development, identities of the languages were only known by the Test and Evaluation team until the date of their release. By June 2021, MATERIAL will release three more languages.

	Languages	Release Date
Program Phase I	Swahili (SWA), Tagalog (TGL)	Oct 2017
	Somali (SOM)	Sep 2018
Program Phase II	Lithuanian (LIT) Bulgarian (BUL)	Mar 2019
	Pashto (PUS)	Jan 2020

Table 1: MATERIAL Languages Released to Date

3. MATERIAL Build Packs

For each program language, IARPA provided to the performer teams a build pack that contained MT and ASR training data. It also included a language specific design document (LSDD) which contains information on dialectal variation within the language, related languages, orthographic variation and Unicode codepoint range. The LSDD also describes domains that were both targeted during data collection and those that were specifically excluded due to difficulty of collecting them. For languages that do not use Latin script, the LSDD provided the corresponding Romanization scheme.

3.1 MT Training Data

The bitext portion of each build pack contained 800,000 words of source language text, carefully translated to English at the sentence level and provided to the performers in the form of parallel sentences. Unlike the main collection for the document partitions described in Section 4, bitext sentences were not restricted to a prescribed set of domains. They were, however, collected from sources similar to those defined by the news text genre, i.e. from news stories and articles. The sets of documents collected for the bitext and the main collection were disjoint.

Source sentences were delivered without any type of editing or spelling normalization. Up to five sentences in sequence taken from a single paragraph in an article were marked to indicate their grouping based on the source article. Content was sourced from widely distributed news stories and articles published by major news outlets and local/regional news stories and articles. No pictures, tables or diagrams were included. Content consisting only of fictional narrative, poetry, political comics or drawings was excluded. Scanned newspaper articles were not accepted, and only content of quality consistent with typical published news stories and articles in the target language was collected. A detailed Data Delivery Specification document was created that included translation guidelines used to manually translate the source-language content into English, including handling of idiomatic expressions and metaphors, numbers, foreign/loan words, titles etc.

Because translation into English was performed at the locations where source-language content was collected, additional quality control steps were performed to ensure that the translations are well-formed and fluent. These included:

- Processing of the English side of bitexts by LanguageTool (Miłkowski, 2010) followed by human review of reported errors of four categories: duplication, grammar, misspelling, and non-conformance. Adding this step to the quality control pipeline significantly improved bitext quality.
- Thorough review by US-based native speakers or trained linguists of random samples of parallel sentences to assess their fluency in idiomatic American English.
- Various automatic and manual checks to ensure adherence to the data delivery specification.

3.2 ASR Training Data

The speech portion of each build pack contained a collection of conversational recordings in the form of 8-bit a-law SPHERE (.sph) files and 24-bit WAVE (.wav) files, together with transcription files encoded as UTF8 text.

The speakers involved in the collection of conversational telephony recordings were required to be native language speakers. They were recruited with the goal of obtaining broad coverage of age, gender, and dialect. They were encouraged to talk about topics they felt most comfortable discussing such as family, friends, sports, movies, etc. These topics were not fixed and varied across languages. Speakers showing distinctive speech disorders were excluded from collection or removed if identified later in the transcription process. All speakers were 18 or older. Dialect regions were defined prior to collection for each language. The number of chosen dialects varied across languages (see Table 2), with no dialect representing less than 10% of the collection.

There were no restrictions on acoustic environment (such as whether or not the speaker was indoors, outdoors, driving, etc.) and this information was provided by the speakers themselves. There were also no restrictions on network specifications or telephone models and these values were also noted in the accompanying metadata. Audio was recorded via telephone over an ISDN connection with a terrestrial telephone network. Each speaker was recorded on a separate channel. No post-processing steps were taken to reduce noise or other artifacts of the recording medium at any stage. The total amount of data for each language is shown in Table 2.

For the sake of transcription, the audio files from both channels were programmatically aligned and merged into a single WAVE file. This reduced the burden on transcribers and produced a single transcription file for each conversation that is separated back into channels for the build pack.

Transcription was performed on short utterances in the audio. Each utterance was transcribed on a new line in the transcription file beginning with a time-stamp that indicates the beginning of the utterance. The time-stamp appears in square brackets. In addition to timestamps, the transcription files may also contain tags to represent speech events such as hesitancies, word fragments, overlap, or prolonged periods of silence. Only the time-stamps, tags, and transcription itself appear in the transcription files. Punctuation in the transcription files was at the discretion of the transcribers who were instructed to abide by natural conventions of the relevant language.

The pronunciation lexicon file provided for each language provides complete coverage of the transcription files in the build pack. The number of terms present in each lexicon is shown in Table 2. This file contains a single term per line with the term in its source language, a Romanized transliteration (where applicable), and a Romanized pronunciation.

Lang	Dialects	Hours	Lex Word Count
SWA	Nairobi	101.92	25289
TGL	North, South, Central	99.94	16129
SOM	Benaadir, Northern	100.29	25874
LIT	Aukstaitian, Samogitian	100.88	32713
BUL	East, West	76.62	22064
PUS	NW, NE, SE, SW	179.77	18745

Table 2: ASR build pack dialects, total hours and word lexicon size per language

4. MATERIAL Documents

For each program language, a document pool was collected of about 15,000 documents with an approximately 3:1 ratio of text to audio documents, in six genres: news text (NT), topical text (TT), and blog text (BT) as well as news broadcast (NB), topical broadcast (TB), and conversational speech (CS). News texts consisted of newswire reports and editorials from national, regional, and local news outlets focusing on news topics and current affairs. These documents targeted a general audience and were presumably highly edited. They were typically around 250-500 words long. Topical texts consisted of articles, reports, non-scientific essays from newspapers or magazines covering a particular topic in-depth. These documents targeted an educated but not specialized audience. They were typically formalized and edited with topic relevant vocabulary and were around 500 words in length. Blog texts were blogs with a single author and did not include discussions or commentaries from other contributors. Blog texts were presumably less edited and more informal with a general vocabulary. They were on average about 500 words. News broadcasts consisted of audio segments of approximately 2.5 minutes from widely distributed broadcasts as well as regional and local news covering news topics and current affairs. The broadcasts were of studio quality while the speech could be formal or informal depending on the segments. Topical broadcasts were similar to news broadcasts in terms of audio quality and speech characteristics but were devoted to in-depth topics and around five minutes in duration. Conversational speech, as described in Section 3.2, consisted of natural conversations between two speakers over the telephone for a duration of approximately 10 minutes on a topic of their choosing from a list of proposed topics. All text and audio documents were five or fewer years old at the time of collection. Outside of checking for the correct language and appropriate content, no additional editing or normalization was performed on these document collections prior to delivery.

Domain	Gloss
Business-And-Commerce (BUS)	All activities and entities associated with economic endeavor.
Government-And-Politics (GOV)	Anything to do with local, regional, national or international government. Includes national level functions such as the provision of national or international infrastructure and capabilities.
Law-And-Order (LAW)	Anything to do with crime, violence or the enforcement of local, regional and national laws.
Lifestyle (LIF)	Anything to do with the lives of families and individuals and the activities they engage in as well as cultural values, norms, practices and expressions.
Military (MIL)	Anything to do with military capability, activity or entities.
Physical-And-Mental-Health (HEA)	Anything to do with the provision of health and wellbeing to a population, as well as causes and correlates that affect health and wellbeing, such as accidents and non-natural disasters. Includes community public health concerns.
Religion (REL)	All aspects of personal and organizational belief systems and practices that relate humanity to what the adherents of that religion consider to be ultimate reality; theological works.
Sports (SPO)	Anything to do with sports activities and entities.

Table 3: Domain names and their glosses

In Phase I of the program, search queries were contextualized by domains, and so the documents were annotated with domain information. While a number of domains were annotated, only eight were eventually released (see Table 3 for their glosses) for the Phase I languages, as listed in Table 4. Annotators were given a gloss for each target domain as well as domain definitions and additional notes to clarify the scope of the domain. Each document had two independent domain annotation passes with a third annotator adjudicating the two previous passes for disagreements.

Lang	Target Domains
SWA	GOV, LIF, BUS, LAW, SPO
TGL	GOV, LIF, HEA, MIL, SPO
SOM	GOV, MIL, BUS, LAW, REL

Table 4: Target domains for the Phase I languages.

The document pool was partitioned into analysis, development, and evaluation sets. The analysis set also included transcriptions and translations of the source documents. It was released to performers months before the official evaluation for glass-box error analysis. Performers were allowed to manually examine the analysis documents in detail and to use it for parameter tuning but were not allowed to mine for or train language models from the vocabulary in the analysis set for their MT/ASR development. Like the analysis set, the development set was also distributed months in advance of the evaluation for internal testing and had the same restrictions as the analysis set. However, unlike the analysis set the development set did not include transcriptions or translations and performers could not manually examine the development documents. The evaluation set for the official evaluation was not released until the start of the evaluation period. Performers were to treat the test set as a blind test set: no examination of the documents, no tuning, no mining for vocabulary.

In Phase I, the partition was based on having the target domains represented in the analysis and development sets in similar frequencies. The evaluation set then would be the remaining documents not selected as the goal was to ensure the target domains and (combinations of target domains) were adequately represented for system development. Additionally, in order to evaluate language identification capabilities of MATERIAL systems, the evaluation set included some distraction data (text and audio documents in a different language than the language being evaluated).

In Phase II, the document partition was changed to focus on achieving a more balanced P_{Rel} (the probability that a document is relevant to the query) across the document sets without any consideration to the domains as domain was dropped from the focus of the Program. Table 5 gives the document volumes for these datasets for the six languages used in the first two phrases of the Program.

Lang	Analysis		Dev		Evaluation	
	Text	Spch	Text	Spch	Text	Spch
SWA	547	266	449	217	10254 (181)	3267 (1043)
TGL	529	315	460	244	10261 (81)	3191 (1260)
SOM	559	279	482	213	10209 (508)	3259 (1383)
LIT	614	215	433	238	10203	3297
BUL	515	312	416	258	10319	3180
PUS	563	284	470	185	10217	3281

Table 5: Document count for the various datasets for the program six target languages. The number in parenthesis denotes the distraction document count.

5. MATERIAL Queries

5.1 Query Typology

Queries are the means by which users express an information need to the CLIR software developed by the performer teams. In contrast to TREC queries, which consist of multiple sentences restating and delimiting the information need, MATERIAL queries are short, consisting of one or two words or short phrases and optional constraints to reduce ambiguity. These come closer to the kinds of queries one might type into a search engine.

The MATERIAL program targets two kinds of requests for information. The first, a **lexical** request, is a request to find documents containing a specific word or phrase (or a translation equivalent of that word or phrase); queries of this type are used to analyze a system's machine translation, speech recognition and retrieval abilities. The second, a **conceptual** request, is a request to find documents related to a specified concept, regardless of which specific words in a given document touch on that concept; queries of this type are used to analyze a system's information retrieval capabilities.

During Phase I of the program, each query was contextualized by one of the target domains for the corresponding language (see Table 4). This means that in order for a query to be relevant to a document, its domain had to match one of the domains assigned to the document, in addition to the document's content matching the query string. In Phase II domains were dropped to simplify both query development and performance analysis. In the remainder of this paper, we discuss queries and their relevance without any additional domain constraints.

A MATERIAL query can consist of one or two requests for information. In the latter case, a document must satisfy both requests in order to be considered relevant. There need not be any relationship between the two requests. We call these queries **conjunction** queries.

Three "in the sense of" semantic constraints were used for queries with ambiguous words or phrases. A synonym (*syn*) constraint specifies an English word or short phrase that conveys approximately the intended sense of the query term (for example, *star [syn: celebrity]*). A hypernym (*hyp*) constraint specifies a superordinate category of the intended sense of the query term (for example, *bat [hyp: animal]*). An event frame (*evf*) constraint specifies the semantic domain of the intended sense of the query term (for example, *bar [evf: nightlife]*).

A subset of program queries was developed to target specific types of information requests that would be challenging for CLIR systems. Phenomena that were hypothesized to be challenging included polysemy (in particular, cases where a specific word in the document language might be translated into English in multiple ways depending on the context in which it is used), homophony (a word in the document language with the same pronunciation as another word in the language), and homography (a word in the document language with the same spelling as an etymologically unrelated word in the language). Additionally, named entities were targeted because they are more likely to be out of vocabulary than non-names, and could be potentially confused with non-named entities.

Below we present MATERIAL query types with a brief explanation of relevance rules and examples (in English, for demonstration purposes). Some examples of **lexical queries** are given below.

Query: *"herbal medicine"*
Type: lexical, single request
What is considered relevant: documents containing [a translation equivalent of] the phrase in the query, including inflectional variants (e.g., *"herbal medicines"*)
Relevant example: Why not try some herbal medicine?
Non-relevant example: Why not try some medicine?

Query: *prisoner, bribery*
Type: lexical, two requests (aka conjunction)
What is considered relevant: documents containing
     [translation equivalents of] both words in the
     query, including inflectional variants, in any order
Relevant example: ...two prisoners escaped ... In
     other news, the mayor is accused of bribery...

Query: *fly [hyp: insect]*
Type: lexical with semantic constraint
What is considered relevant: documents containing [a
     translation equivalent of] the specified sense of the
     word in the query
Relevant example: There's a fly in my soup!
Non-relevant example: Kiwis can't fly.

The program has also developed a special subtype of
lexical queries called **morphological** queries. Queries of
this type targeted words with specific marked (e.g., non-
default) morphological properties. For example, the query
<will tell> would match only forms of '*tell*' (or a
translation equivalent of this word) in the future tense. (In
contrast, the [non-morphological] lexical query *tell* would
match forms of '*tell*' in any tense.) Another example of a
morphological query is given below.

Query: *<prisoners>*
Type: lexical (morphological)
What is considered relevant: documents containing [a
     translation equivalent of] the word in the query
     with the same marked morphological features as
     the word in the query (in this case, plural number)
Relevant example: prisoners escaped
Non-relevant example: only one prisoner died

A **conceptual** query contains a conceptual request for
information. General conceptual requests are marked with
a plus sign: *"violence in Sudan"+*. An additional kind of
conceptual request was used called **EXAMPLE_OF**. This
kind of request was used to test a system's knowledge of
basic/natural class hierarchies. A document was considered
relevant if it mentioned a subtype of the specified concept.
For example, a document would be considered relevant to
the request *EXAMPLE_OF(apparel)* if it mentioned
sweaters; if the document only contained the word
'*apparel*' (or a translation equivalent thereof), it would not
be considered relevant. EXAMPLE_OF requests have been
discontinued for the third period of performance.

A distinction is made between "pure" conceptual queries,
which consist of a single conceptual request, and "hybrid"
conceptual queries, which contain/conjoin one conceptual
request and one lexical request. For practical reasons,
queries consisting of two conceptual requests are
disallowed. Some examples of conceptual queries are given
below.

Query: *"violence in Sudan"+*
Type: conceptual, single request (pure conceptual)
What is considered relevant: documents that touch on
     the specified concept
Relevant example: Negotiations in Sudan ended
     abruptly after violent clashes erupted in the capital.
Non-relevant example: Protesters in Sudan marched
     outside the presidential palace in Khartoum.

Query: *EXAMPLE_OF(freshwater fish)*
Type: conceptual (EXAMPLE_OF)
What is considered relevant: documents mentioning a
     subtype of the requested concept
Relevant example: I caught a carp
Non-relevant example: A large catch of cod

Query: *strike+ [evf: labor]*
Type: conceptual with semantic constraint
What is considered relevant: documents that touch on
     the specified sense of the requested concept
Relevant example: Teachers staged a walkout
Non-relevant example: Threat of a terrorist attack

Query: *"traditional practice", health+*
Type: conceptual, hybrid/conjunction
What is considered relevant: documents that contain [a
     translation equivalent of] the lexical phrase in the
     query and touch on the specified concept
Relevant example: A traditional practice in the
     Philippines is to use guava leaf ointment to
     expedite healing.
Non-relevant example: Guava leaf tea tastes terrible.

5.2 Query Development and Annotation Process

Queries were developed by teams of three native language
speakers per language. They input queries into a web-based
tool called the Query Development Tool (QDT) which was
developed from scratch to support this effort. This tool was
used to develop and test queries against document sets as
well as to annotate relevance judgments for individual
documents. The QDT also allowed for quality control
checks at several stages in the process.

Inspiration for queries came from a variety of sources.
Using the QDT, query developers could retrieve a random
text or speech document and look for content that might
make an interesting query. Some queries were developed
from wordlists derived from program documents, such as
topical words extracted via Latent Dirichlet Allocation
(McCallum, 2002). Often, while annotating one query, a
query developer might encounter information in a
document that would serve as the basis for their next query.
Many queries were based on ideas that came directly from
the query developer (for example, the developer might
think of a word that happens to be a homograph, and use
that as the basis for a query).

Once a query developer had a query concept in mind, they
created a list of specially formulated QDT queries that were
used to find all documents that could possibly be relevant
to the query, including the English query string. QDT
searches were intended to achieve 100% recall of relevant
documents; precision was not a factor at this stage.

Queries were later reviewed by a second native language
speaker, as well as a native English speaker. The vetting
process included checks that queries met a number of
different criteria, including: 1) Is the query well-formed? 2)
Is the query clear for a native speaker of English? 3) Is the
query specific enough, or do constraints need to be added?
4) Does the QDT search contain all possible translation

equivalents of the query? 5) Does the QDT search account for all possible inflected forms of words in the query? 6) Does the query correspond to relevant documents? If a query did not meet the quality control targets, it was either further refined or discarded. Once the native speaker and the English speaker reviewers agreed that the query met the vetting criteria, the query was marked as "frozen" in the QDT, and no further query edits were made.

After queries were vetted, the initial query developer annotated documents in the corpus according to their relevance to the query. For lexical queries, if any lexical item in a particular document was a translational equivalent to the query term, the document was marked as relevant. For conceptual queries, a relevant document did not need to contain an exact translation equivalent of the query term(s), but it had to cover the query topic. The QDT showed query developers snippets of documents containing words that matched parts of the search. In some cases, particularly with lexical queries, the snippets provided were not sufficient for the annotator to determine whether the query was relevant; in those cases, annotators could click on the set of snippets and be shown the entire document, with items matching QDT search terms. Following document annotation, a second round of vetting took place before the query was finalized.

5.3 Query Statistics

Table 6 and Table 7 show total counts of various query types developed for each language against text and speech documents, respectively. All queries were partitioned into two disjoint subsets: Q1 was a set of queries annotated against development and analysis document partitions and were released to the performers together with those document partitions. Q2 was a set of queries annotated against the evaluation partitions and were used to evaluate system performance. The two tables list the four basic query types, lexical, morphological, conceptual and EXAMPLE_OF, as well as their conjunctions. The average P_{Rel} (see Section 4) for these query sets is 0.00165.

6. MATERIAL Evaluation Metric

The nominal MATERIAL use case is one in which a user is monitoring a stream of documents for topics of interest. A perfect system would detect all the relevant documents, while rejecting all the non-relevant ones. In practice, some relevant documents will be missed and some non-relevant ones will be falsely detected. Given that scenario, the primary MATERIAL performance metric was designed to allow the program to measure the trade-off that systems are making between miss rates and false alarm rates.

This measure, called QV (Query Value), is defined for a given query as:

$$QV = 1 - P_{Miss} - \beta \cdot P_{FA}$$

where P_{Miss} is the probability that a relevant document for the query will not be detected, and P_{FA} is the probability that a non-relevant document will be incorrectly detected.

		SWA	TGL	SOM	LIT	BUL	PUS
l	Q1	93	54	112	131	56	60
	Q2	351	360	408	495	247	162
m	Q1	6	5	12	29	11	10
	Q2	91	51	75	113	54	22
c	Q1	9	8	3	2	23	3
	Q2	27	111	11	5	67	14
e	Q1	10	1	0	2	2	1
	Q2	8	28	9	21	7	2
l,l	Q1	33	36	34	15	87	93
	Q2	226	149	99	53	307	254
l,m	Q1	0	1	3	6	17	24
	Q2	8	11	28	15	49	69
m,m	Q1	0	0	0	0	0	0
	Q2	1	0	0	1	0	0
l,c	Q1	21	17	35	74	51	79
	Q2	247	76	289	239	179	202
m,c	Q1	0	0	0	0	0	0
	Q2	0	1	0	0	4	0
l,e	Q1	0	2	4	15	23	6
	Q2	10	10	37	38	72	18

Table 6: Number of queries of different types developed against **speech** documents in each language. Q1 and Q2 are query sets against Development+Analysis and Evaluation document partitions, respectively. l, m, c, and e stand for lexical, morphological, conceptual and EXAMPLE_OF query types, respectively.

		SWA	TGL	SOM	LIT	BUL	PUS
l	Q1	67	36	82	74	29	34
	Q2	314	321	346	390	198	116
m	Q1	4	5	13	12	6	5
	Q2	66	44	60	87	36	11
c	Q1	8	3	1	1	10	0
	Q2	22	106	8	2	39	2
e	Q1	9	3	0	2	1	0
	Q2	8	29	8	11	6	2
l,l	Q1	19	20	24	4	46	39
	Q2	194	125	78	34	222	160
l,m	Q1	0	0	1	3	8	7
	Q2	7	11	26	9	34	31
m,m	Q1	0	0	0	0	0	0
	Q2	0	0	0	1	0	0
l,c	Q1	19	10	17	30	22	21
	Q2	159	55	211	133	101	69
m,c	Q1	0	0	0	0	0	0
	Q2	0	0	0	0	4	0
l,e	Q1	0	2	3	9	13	2
	Q2	6	9	22	25	46	5

Table 7: Number of queries of different types developed against **text** documents in each language. Q1 and Q2 are query sets against Development+Analysis and Evaluation document partitions, respectively. l, m, c, and e stand for lexical, morphological, conceptual and EXAMPLE_OF query types, respectively.

The parameter β is defined as:

$$\beta = \frac{C}{V} \cdot \left(\frac{1}{P_{Rel}} - 1 \right)$$

where C is the cost of an incorrect detection and V is the value of a correct detection.

In MATERIAL all queries are equally weighted and so the program metric Actual Weighted Query Value (AQWV) is the simple average over all the QVs for a system operating at its actual detection threshold. In any given evaluation, the MATERIAL Test and Evaluation Team specifies β as a constant *a priori*, and performer systems optimize their performance accordingly. A typical value of β is 40 ($V = 1$, $C = 0.0668$, $P_{rel} = 0.0017$). Because of the equal weighting of queries, AQWV is better suited than many traditional information retrieval metrics for the needle-in-the-haystack MATERIAL system use case.

Note that $AQWV = 1.0$ for a perfect system; $AQWV = 0$ for a system that detects no documents at all; and, $AQWV = -\beta$ if all the detected documents are false alarms.

Table 8 shows maximal AQWV CLIR scores achieved by individual MATERIAL performer systems on the speech and text portions of the evaluation sets for five of the six program languages evaluated as of March 2020.

Language	Beta	Mode	AQWV CLIR
SWA	20	speech	0.4556
		text	0.5046
TGL	20	speech	0.5917
		text	0.6408
SOM	40	speech	0.2036
		text	0.2901
LIT	40	speech	0.6093
		text	0.6497
BUL	40	speech	0.6539
		text	0.7244

Table 8: Maximal single-system CLIR AQWV for the MATERIAL languages evaluated as of March 2020.

7. Summary

In this paper we presented several document and query datasets that were created by the IARPA MATERIAL research program for development of CLIR and summarization systems for six LRLs and provided details on document collection and annotation as well as query development, annotation and vetting. The program has propelled research in these areas yielding, as of March 2020, almost 100 publications by the performer teams. The datasets described in this paper are currently being released to US Government entities. It has not been determined if or when they could also be released to a wider research community.

8. Acknowledgements

We thank the anonymous reviewers for helpful comments. This effort is supported by the Office of the Director of National Intelligence (ODNI), Intelligence Advanced Research Projects Activity (IARPA), via contracts 2019-19022100010-005, 2018-1701100005-001, FA8702-15-D-0001, FA8702-15-D-0001, and D2017-1708030008. The views and conclusions contained herein are those of the authors and should not be interpreted as necessarily representing the official policies, either expressed or implied, of ODNI, IARPA, or the U.S. Government. The U.S. Government is authorized to reproduce and distribute reprints for governmental purposes notwithstanding any copy-right annotation therein.

9. Bibliographical References

Ferro, N., & Peters, C. (2019). From multilingual to multimodal: the evolution of CLEF over two decades. In *Information Retrieval Evaluation in a Changing World* (pp. 3-44). Springer, Cham.

Harper, M. (2011). Babel Broad Agency Announcement. https://www.iarpa.gov/index.php/research-programs/babel/baa

McCallum, A. K. (2002). Mallet: A machine learning for language toolkit. http://mallet.cs.umass.edu

Miłkowski, M. (2010). Developing an open-source, rule-based proofreading tool. *Software: Practice and Experience*, 40(7), 543-566.

Rubino, C. (2017). Material Broad Agency Announcement. https://www.iarpa.gov/index.php/research-programs/material/material-baa

Voorhees, E. M., & Harman, D. K. (Eds.). (2005). *TREC: Experiment and evaluation in information retrieval* (Vol. 63). Cambridge: MIT press.

Proceedings of the Cross-Language Search and Summarization of Text and Speech Workshop, pages 14–21
Language Resources and Evaluation Conference (LREC 2020), Marseille, 11–16 May 2020
© European Language Resources Association (ELRA), licensed under CC-BY-NC

MATERIALizing Cross-Language Information Retrieval: A Snapshot

Petra Galuščáková[1], Douglas W. Oard[1], Joseph Barrow[1], Suraj Nair[1], Han-Chin Shing[1],
Elena Zotkina[1], Ramy Eskander,[2] and Rui Zhang[3]
[1] University of Maryland, College Park, MD; [2] Columbia University, New York, NY; [3] Yale University, New Haven, CT
petra@umd.edu

Abstract

At about the midpoint of the IARPA MATERIAL program in October 2019, an evaluation was conducted on systems' abilities to find Lithuanian documents based on English queries. Subsequently, both the Lithuanian test collection and results from all three teams were made available for detailed analysis. This paper capitalizes on that opportunity to begin to look at what's working well at this stage of the program, and to identify some promising directions for future work.

Keywords: information, retrieval, evaluation

1. Introduction

To some extent, research on Cross-Language Information Retrieval (CLIR) has repeatedly been a casualty of its own success. Research in the 1970's focused on extending monolingual thesauri to multilingual thesauri. Although there were some issues to address involving the ways conceptual differences were reflected in different cultures (and thus in different languages), the thesaurus-based retrieval systems of the day proved to be relatively easily extended to include entry vocabulary from different languages. Thus, after publication of an ISO multilingual thesaurus standard in 1986 there was little further research left to do along those lines (Oard and Diekema, 1998). The 1990's saw the rapid development of a different paradigm for CLIR, one in which queries were expressed in natural language and the system's goal was to rank, not to select, documents. Much of the initial work focused on dictionary-based techniques and on techniques based on comparable corpora, but it was the introduction of techniques based on parallel text around the turn of the century that essentially solved the cross-language ranking problem (Nie, 2010). Of course, ranking is only useful in interactive applications if the searcher can recognize relevant documents, so success with cross-language ranking led to a continuation of ranked retrieval CLIR research in the first decade of the twenty-first century that focused on the ability of machine translation to support cross-language relevance assessment (Gonzalo and Oard, 2004). Results there were promising as well, even with the limited capabilities of the translation technology of the day, and there the research story largely ends, with attention then shifting to deployment of the technology in applications such as 2lingual[1].

The first two waves of CLIR research were driven by language resources: by thesauri in the first wave, and by CLIR test collections in the second. With the genesis of the IARPA MATERIAL program in 2016 (Rubino, 2016), we now find ourselves at the vanguard of a third wave of CLIR research, one that draws on ideas from the first two, while adding two new twists. Like the first wave, the goal of MATERIAL is not to rank but rather to choose. Like the second wave, the goal is not just to automate the process but to get the human in the loop. Two additional issues for MATERIAL are evident from its name: Machine Translation for English Retrieval of Information in Any Language. One is a broader focus on information rather than text, with both text and speech in the same test collection. The other is a focus on affordable application to any language, even those with limited language resources.

In this paper, we focus most strongly on MATERIAL's focus on choice over ranking. MATERIAL queries are not simply a bag of words, as was typical of second-wave CLIR test collections. Rather, a MATERIAL query is a logical form, specifying what should be found, and the items to be returned (text documents or speech recordings) are all and only those that are logically entailed by the query. If this were a thought experiment, it would be reminiscent of Cooper's pioneering work on logical relevance (Cooper, 1971). But it is not a thought experiment; MATERIAL's focus is on the empirical realization of that vision. Our goal in this paper is to begin to look, at one point in time, at how well that has yet been done, both with an eye towards assessing where we are, and also with an eye towards envisioning possible future directions.

The perspective that we draw on for this paper is based on the exchange of document-level results from all three MATERIAL teams for an evaluation of Lithuanian text and speech retrieval that was conducted in October, 2019[2]. As is common in information retrieval evaluation, aggregate measures for these three runs were reported soon after the runs were submitted. Our focus here, however, is not principally on aggregate measures, but on individual cases:

- What patterns are evident in what was found?

- What patterns are evident in what was not found by any team?

- What happened when there was nothing to be found?

- And, how much better can we do if we have access to different ways of finding things?

---

[1] https://www.2lingual.com/

[2] This data has not been released publicly.

The paper is organized as follows: first we provide a broad overview of the types of approaches used by the three participating teams, providing individual references for additional details. Sections 3 and 4 provide answers to the four questions raised above. Finally, we conclude the paper with some remarks on next steps.

2. CLIR Systems

All three teams employ complex architectures that generally combine several processing approaches. Each of the teams includes one or more automatic speech recognition (ASR) techniques, and one or more machine translation (MT) approaches, all developed specifically for the MATERIAL task. As each team uses their own data for ASR and MT training, these systems thus not only differ in the approaches used, but also in the training data. Moreover, each team creates different variants of retrieval systems, which not only differ in the applied ASR and MT, but also in their text processing (lemmatization, stemming, character normalization, etc.) and query processing (synonym and hypernym processing, phrase processing, etc.) techniques. Retrieval systems also differ in the ways they transfer the queries and documents into a shared space. Either the English queries can be translated into Lithuanian, the Lithuanian documents can be translated into English, or queries and documents can be transformed into some other shared space (e.g., using embeddings). Evidence from multiple systems can also be combined by a variety of methods. Available data sources can be combined before retrieval, evidence from different systems can be combined during the matching phase, or the documents retrieved by different systems can be combined after the matching phase. Details on the approaches used by the SARAL team are described in (Boschee et al., 2019), the approaches used by the FLAIR team are described in (Zbib et al., 2019; Zhao et al., 2019), and the approaches used by the SCRIPTS team are described in (Oard et al., 2019).

3. Experiments

3.1. Corpus Description

The IARPA MATERIAL corpus currently consists of document collections in six languages: Swahili, Tagalog, Somali, Lithuanian, Bulgarian, and Pashto. Our analysis is based on the Lithuanian collection, for which we have results from all three participating teams. Collection statistics are given in Table 1. Details of the collection and the annotation process can be found in (Zavorin et al., 2020).

Queries There are 1,000 English queries in the collection. The queries are written in the MATERIAL Query Language (MQL), which is specified using a context-free grammar. There are three basic query types: simple, conceptual, and conjunction. Simple queries (also called lexical queries) are queries with either single word or a single phrase. A simple query "requests the system to find documents that contain a translation equivalent of the query string. A translation equivalent should sound natural to a native speaker" (NIST, 2016). Simple queries can have one of three types of semantic constraints: synonym, hypernym,

or event frame. Simple queries can also have morphological constraints, where the term must match morphological features of the query string (e.g., past tense on verbs; plural on nouns). One type of conceptual query (indicated by a plus sign) is similar to a TREC query, asking for documents on a topic. Another type of conceptual query is the "example of" operator, which asks for documents which provide specific examples for the query terms. Conjunctive queries require the presence of two query parts. When one of those parts is conceptual, the conjunctive query is referred to as hybrid. We count the number of queries with each feature in Table 2.

Document Genres The corpus contains both text documents and speech recordings, which can be further subdivided by the source. There are a total of 10,203 text documents and 3,297 speech recordings, each modality being broken into 3 different genres. Documents (a term used inclusively in MATERIAL to refer to both text documents and speech recordings) are thus provided in six genres (NIST, 2016):

1. News Text (Text) - newswire or reports. Formal language.

2. Topical Text (Text) - specialty articles or reports. Diverse language formality.

3. Social Media/Blogs (Text) - blogs. Language less formal/edited.

4. News Broadcasts (Speech) - formal spoken language.

5. Topical Broadcasts (Speech) - diverse language formality.

6. Conversational Speech (Speech) - generally informal spoken language.

The amounts of Topical Text and News Text documents are similar, and each is almost three times larger than the amount of Social Media/Blog content. Similarly, the amounts of News Broadcast and Topical Broadcast recordings are similar, and about two times larger than the amount of Conversational Speech.

3.2. Official Results

We refer to the three participating systems as Teams A, B, and C to preserve anonymity. A comparison of scores for each team from the October 2019 evaluation is shown in Table 3. AQWV is the official program measure (NIST, 2016). Although the program objective is set-based retrieval, documents returned by each team also have a confidence score that can be used as a basis for ranking. This enables us to compute Mean Average Precision (MAP) on the returned list of documents, although we note that different systems return different numbers of relevant documents so the MAP values may not be strictly comparable. MQWV is an AQWV variant calculated for an optimal threshold, which is in our case determined by using either an optimal confidence score cutoff (MQWV threshold) or an optimal rank cutoff (MQWV rank) that is tied across all queries. System ordering is the same for each of the four measures.

Modality	Source	Query Type (# of judgements)			Total Documents
		Lexical	Conceptual	Hybrid	
Text	Blogs	1,225	25	181	1,491
	Topical	5,755	106	1,032	4,094
	News	3,922	65	648	4,618
Speech	Conversational	90	1	8	613
	Broadcast	1,008	11	13	1,334
	Topical	1,402	8	189	1,350
Total Queries		691	26	283	

Table 1: Corpus statistics for the IARPA MATERIAL Lithuanian evaluation collection.

Query Feature	# of queries	example
simple	974	"sculpture park"
conjunction	353	cold[hyp:sickness],tea
hybrid	283	"keep balance","physical exercise"+
plus sign (conceptual)	249	"copper in food"+
synonym constrint	180	telescope[syn:optical instrument]
morphology constraint	134	"<won> a prize"
hypernym constraint	130	cinnamon[hyp:spice]
example of	60	EXAMPLE_OF(baggage)
event frame constraint	34	conductor[evf:music]

Table 2: Numbers of queries with different features. We consider each of several query features independently. A query such as *lobster,EXAMPLE_OF(shellfish)* would be counted as: a hybrid query, a simple query, a conceptual query, and an example of query.

3.3. Comparison by Query Feature

Because conceptual, simple, and hybrid queries can overlap, we instead look at results by individual *features*, as opposed to query *types*.

The feature with the greatest number of queries is "simple" (974/1,000 queries contain a "simple" component), whereas only 34 queries have an event frame constraint. In Figure 1, we present both MAP and AQWV per query feature. Because of the imbalance in representation of each feature, performing better across a majority of features does not necessarily imply performing the best over all queries. We see this in Figure 1(a), where Team A performs the best across nearly all features, but marginally lower than Team C on queries with "simple" features. In general, conceptual and hybrid queries are difficult for all teams (those with the "plus_sign", "example_of", or "hybrid" feature). Results across queries with these features are much lower than for simple queries.

Figure 1 presents both a ranking metric (MAP) and a set-based retrieval metric (AQWV), which give different insights into the systems. AQWV introduces a penalty for returning too many documents, and it thus requires both finding relevant documents and selecting a good cutoff on a per-query basis. Though MAP and AQWV behave similarly for cumulative results (Table 3) and they similarly predict the "hardness" of the query features in Figure 1, the relative ordering of the teams in terms of AQWV and MAP scores often differ (for example Team A outperforms Team C on conceptual queries ("plus_sign") on text in terms of MAP

but Team C actually does a bit better in terms of AQWV). The ordering of the teams in terms of the MAP and AQWV cumulative scores is also in line with the results achieved by both versions of the MQWV measure. Though the score cutoffs cannot be directly compared across the teams as the teams use different score normalization methods, the optimal ranks show that the optimal number of returned documents is the same for teams A and C and it is slightly smaller for team B. Identical optimal ranks for teams A and C also allow us to compare the ranking of these two systems and indicate that team B is doing slightly better in ranking of text documents.

3.4. Document-Level Analysis

Breakdown by Document Types Numbers of retrieved and relevant documents broken down into the document types is in the Table 4. In general, Team A achieves a higher precision and slightly lower recall, while Team B and C achieve a higher recall and a lower precision. Importantly, these result do not translate directly to AQWV, as AQWV is an average across the queries, not across the retrieved documents.

The proportion of the retrieved document types is similar across the three teams, and it differs from the proportion of the collection document types. The ratio of returned blog documents is for each team smaller than the ratio of blog text in the collection (ranging from 9 to 10%, as opposed to 15%), similarly to the ratio of news text (ranging from 33 to 36%, as opposed to 45%), while the ratio of the returned topical text is larger for each team (ranging from

	Text			Speech		
	Team A	Team B	Team C	Team A	Team B	Team C
AQWV	0.617	0.609	**0.650**	**0.609**	0.600	0.605
MQWV threshold	0.619	0.617	**0.650**	**0.616**	0.603	0.605
MQWV rank	0.622 (40)	0.572 (35)	**0.634** (40)	**0.614** (13)	0.550 (10)	0.612 (12)
MAP	0.547	0.513	**0.552**	**0.596**	0.566	0.581

Table 3: Performance of the teams in the evaluation for text and speech. The highest value for each measure for text/speech is in a bold. For MQWV rank we also provide the optimal rank cutoff (in the parentheses).

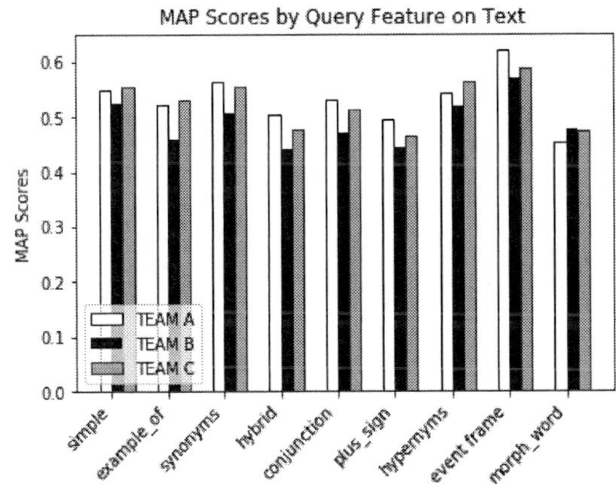

(a) MAP scores on text broken down by query feature.

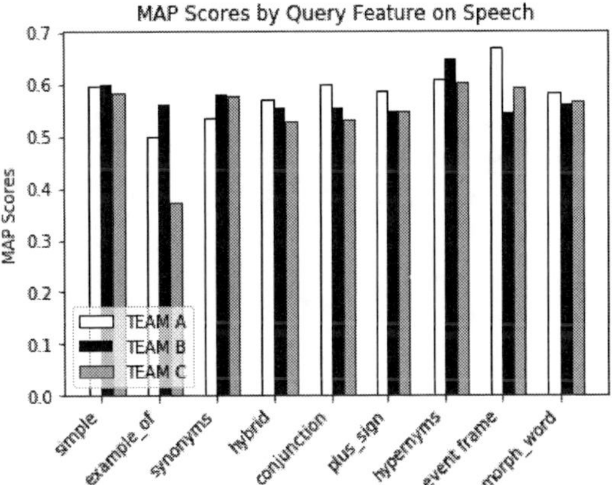

(b) MAP scores on speech broken down by query feature.

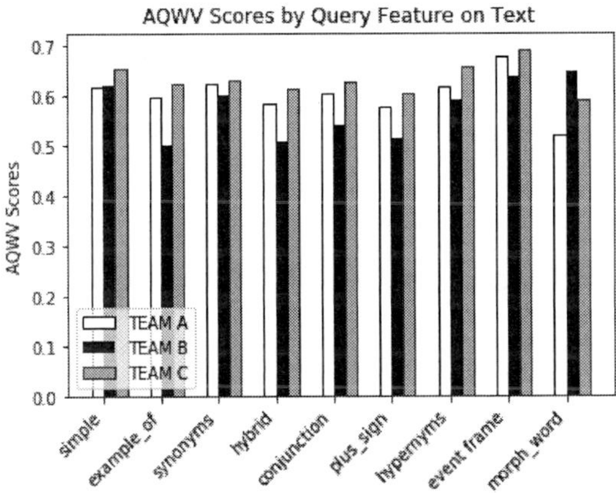

(c) AQWV scores on text broken down by query feature.

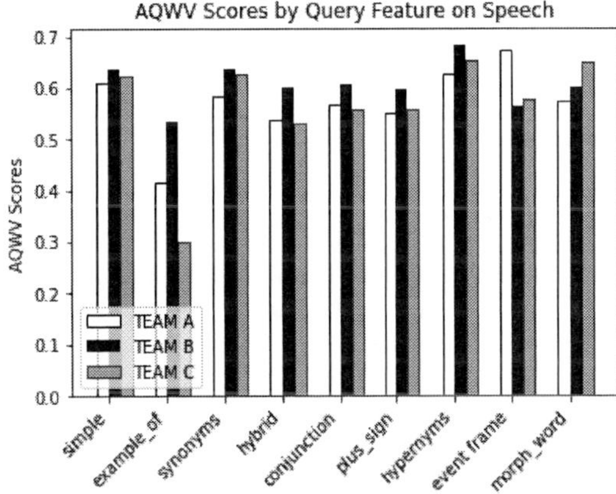

(d) AQWV scores on speech broken down by query feature.

Figure 1: Dependence of the MAP and AQWV score on different query features for each team.

54 to 57%, as opposed to 40% in the collection). The trend is similar in speech, with conversational speech documents forming only 2 to 5% of the returned documents (the ratio of conversational speech in the collection is 19%), and topical broadcast which is for Teams A and B 61% and 57% of the returned documents respectively (compared to 41% of the documents in the collection). However, the proportion of retrieved documents corresponds well with the number of relevant documents of different types (text: 11% of blog, 53% of topical and 36% of news; speech: 4% of conversational, 38% of broadcast and 59% of topical).

Breakdown by Document Length Diverse ranking approaches utilized by different teams might lead to different biases with regard to particular length. The length of the documents retrieved at each position for each team is presented in Figure 2, together with the average length of the relevant documents. These results imply that teams A and B return documents somewhat longer than the average relevant document for both text and speech. Teams A and C show some bias towards returning longer documents first in text.

Missed Documents We investigate the number of relevant documents found and missed by each team, in rela-

		# Relevant / # Retrieved (Precision)		
		Team A	Team B	Team C
Text	Blogs	995 / 3,167 (31%)	1,080 / 4,035 (27%)	1,109 / 4,592 (24%)
	Topical	5,172 / 19,533 (27%)	5,495 / 21,519 (26%)	5,452 / 24,704 (22%)
	News	3,482 / 11,256 (31%)	3,775 / 12,962 (29%)	3,702 / 16,426 (23%)
Speech	Conversational	61 / 216 (28%)	72 / 468 (15%)	53 / 471 (11%)
	Broadcast	863 / 3,329 (26%)	854 / 3,258 (26%)	911 / 6,005 (15%)
	Topical	1,220 / 5,554 (22%)	1,177 / 4,937 (24%)	1,209 / 7,799 (16%)

Table 4: Here we break down the types of documents being returned by each team.

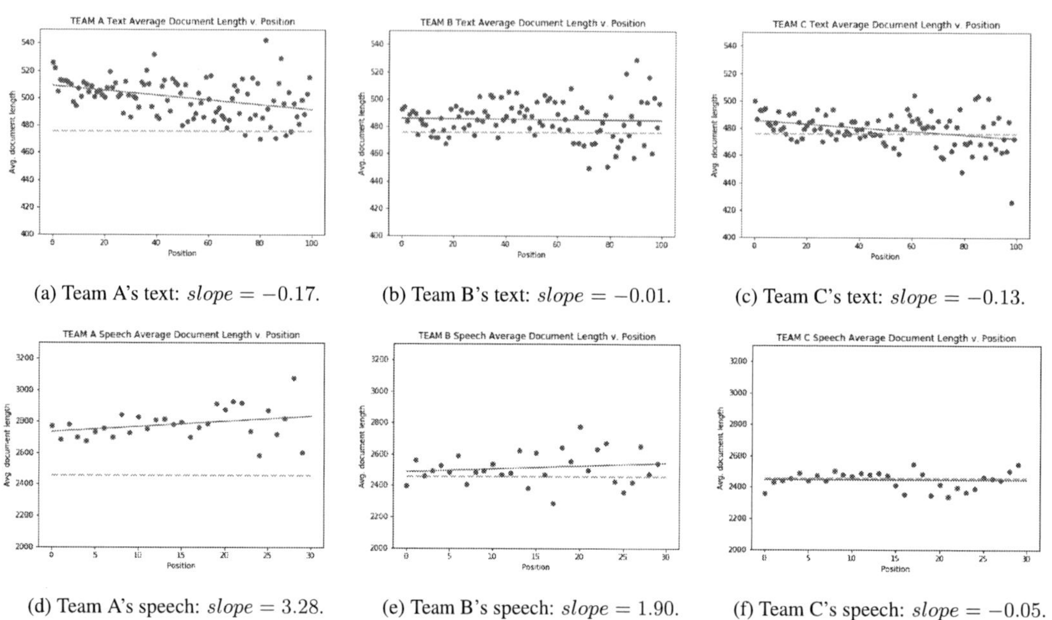

(a) Team A's text: $slope = -0.17$.

(b) Team B's text: $slope = -0.01$.

(c) Team C's text: $slope = -0.13$.

(d) Team A's speech: $slope = 3.28$.

(e) Team B's speech: $slope = 1.90$.

(f) Team C's speech: $slope = -0.05$.

Figure 2: For each team and modality, we plot the average document length in words returned at each position, over all 1,000 queries. For text, we look at the first 100 positions, and for speech the first 30. The solid line is a linear regression over the plot, and the dashed line is the average *relevant* document length for the modality. A negative slope implies that the team is biased towards returning longer documents at higher positions, whereas a flat slope implies an independence between position and length.

tionship to each other (Table 5). All teams found 8,255 relevant text documents (of a possible 12,959) and 1,620 speech documents (of a possible 2,900). The more interesting documents, however, are the ones that all teams missed (1,258 text documents and 332 speech documents). We additionally stratify the analysis by the number of documents that each single team found or missed that both of the other teams missed or found. These results indicate that Team A is the least diverse with respect to teams B and C, as the number of the correctly retrieved exclusively by A is the smallest and the number of relevant documents missed exclusively by A is the largest. Deeper analysis of the missed documents is described next. To complement the one-v-all breakdown in Table 5, we also provide the number of found/missed documents for each team independently (Table 6).

3.5. Failure Analysis

To identify opportunities for improvement, we examined relevant documents that no team retrieved and grouped those documents into categories that seem to us to be potentially useful for explaining those failures. Because there are more such documents than we could examine, we used two sampling strategies. In one approach, we first selected queries that all teams performed relatively poorly on by sorting based on average precision, selecting queries with the lowest values, and examining all documents that were missed by every team for such queries. We augmented this set with some random selection among documents missed by all teams for other queries in order to avoid focusing exclusively on a narrow range of queries. To investigate why a relevant document was missed, we search for the translations of query term(s) using the mapping learned from a parallel corpus. If we are unable to find it, then we manu-

		Teams B + C (Text / Speech)	
		found	missed
Team A	found	8,255 / 1,620	203 / 80
	missed	2,052 / 424	1,258 / 332
		Teams A + C (Text / Speech)	
Team B	found	8,255 / 1,620	650 / 140
	missed	1,351 / 465	1,258 / 332
		Teams A + B (Text / Speech)	
Team C	found	8,255 / 1,620	542 / 116
	missed	1,438 / 395	1,258 / 332

Table 5: Paired comparison of found and missed documents per team.

ally inspect the English translation of the relevant document obtained using our trained machine translation system. As a last resort, we inspect the Google Translate output for the relevant document. The following sections describe some of the systematic error patterns.

3.5.1. Missed translations

There exist several queries for which the relevant documents do not contain the exact query word but rather synonyms of it. For the query *diffidence*, the relevant documents contain translations of *shyness* and *modesty*, which are synonyms of the query word *diffidence*. Similarly for the query *faucet*, an unfound relevant document contains a translation of the word *tap*. Other examples are the queries *futility*, *futility,hope+*, *jello[syn:gelatin dessert]*, *ditch[syn:a trench]*, *prank[syn:a joke]* and *"Christmas ornament"*, where the system does not match them against documents whose translations contain *pointlessness*, *jelly*, *trench*, *joke* and *"Christmas toy"*, respectively. Some of the unfound translations might by found by matching the stem rather than the word. Considering the query *truck[syn:lorry]*, the relevant document contains a translation of *trucks*, which can be stemmed to find the query word *truck*. Another case is the query *EXAMPLE_OF(ground transportation),"commute to work"*, where the relevant document contains a translation of the phrase *"commuting to worker"*. A much harder example is the query *psaltery*, which never occurs in a parallel corpus that we examined, and thus might require some form of expansion to be able to identify the correct translation (kanklės, a Baltic psaltery instrument).

3.5.2. Translation ambiguity

Queries with semantic constraints (synonym, hypernym or event frame) require the system to be able to find the documents that match the correct sense of the query word. For the semantically constrained query, *bachelor[syn:unmarried man]*, the documents returned mention *bachelor's degree* instead of *unmarried man*.

3.5.3. EXAMPLE_OF queries

Systems missed some documents for conceptual queries due to incomplete expansion. The relevant document for the query *"spoiled EXAMPLE_OF(food)"* contains the translation of the phrase *"spoiled shrimp"*. The system needs to correctly expand the query to include *shrimp* as an example of food. Relevant documents for the query *"EXAMPLE_OF(natural resource) mine"* contain the translations of hyponyms of a natural resource; *gold*, *coal*, *uranium*, *lime* and *mint*. These hyponyms might be obtained by expanding the queries using external knowledge sources such as WordNet or by exploiting word embeddings.

3.5.4. Term proximity

For the query *"cause of death",contamination+*, a relevant document contains the translation of the phrase *cause of increasing human mortality*. The challenge here is to recognize *mortality* as the synonym of query word *death* and to be able to match an entire phrase that extends beyond the length of the query phrase. In this case, Sequential Dependence Model (Metzler and Croft, 2005) might be a good choice to capture long-term dependencies.

3.5.5. Morphological constraints

Queries with morphological constraint requires the machine translation systems to correctly translate the document terms preserving the root morphological aspect. For query *<squandered>*, the document is missed since the MT system incorrectly translates the relevant document term to *squandering*. In another example, the document translation produced by MT system contains *shall comfort* which does not entirely match the original query *<will comfort>*, causing the retrieval system to rank it lower.

3.5.6. Incorrect judgements

Each of the systems miss the relevant documents for the query *mistletoe,EXAMPLE_OF(bird)*. On manually inspecting the relevant documents, however, we were not able to find the translation of query word *mistletoe* in them. This might be a case of an erroneous judgement.

3.5.7. Incomplete judgements

For query *volcano*, the documents returned by the systems which are marked as non-relevant contain the word *vulkanas* (translation of volcano). However, it happens to be the name of a football team instead of a volcanic eruption. Technically, these documents should be marked relevant as there are no constraints that require the query term to match the sense of volcanic eruption.

3.6. Number of returned documents

Comparison of the numbers of retrieved documents by different teams is in Table 7. The system from Team C returns the highest number of documents on average, and returns documents for the most queries. The average variance of the number of returned documents is highest for the Team B. We additionally consider the number of queries for which the systems *correctly* returned no documents. For text, that number is low across all three teams; when a system returns no documents, that is the correct choice between 0% and 8% of the time. For speech, all teams tend not to return any documents in more cases, which corresponds well with the smaller number of relevance judgements available for the speech documents (see Table 1). The amount of correctly judged empty queries is in speech notably higher, between 56% and 67%.

		Team A	Team B	Team C	All
Relevant	found	9,649 / 2,144	10,350 / 2,103	10,263 / 2,173	8,255 / 1,620
	missed	3,310 / 756	2,609 / 797	2,696 / 727	4,704 / 1,280

Table 6: Numbers of found and missed relevant documents per team (text/speech modality).

	Text			Speech		
	Team A	Team B	Team C	Team A	Team B	Team C
Avg. # returned docs	34	39	46	9	9	14
Std. Dev. of # returned docs	38	55	31	10	14	11
Total # of queries with no returned docs	39	40	1	90	139	6
Total # of *correctly* empty queries	3	2	0	50	83	4

Table 7: Statistics of the number of documents returned by the submitted systems, broken down into text and speech.

4. System Combination

Post-retrieval combination of multiple systems often leads to improved results on both mono-lingual and cross-lingual information retrieval (Lee, 1997; Shaw and Fox, 1994; Karakos et al., 2013; Shing et al., 2019). We implement MAJORITY VOTE and COMBMNZ (Shaw and Fox, 1994) to combine the results from three teams. See Table 8 for the combination results.

		P_{miss}	P_{FA}	AQWV
Text	Single Best	0.211	0.00348	0.650
	Majority Vote	0.243	0.00183	0.684
	STO CombMNZ	0.194	0.00279	0.695
	MinMax CombMNZ	0.185	0.00277	**0.704**
Speech	Single Best	0.306	0.00211	0.609
	Majority Vote	0.251	0.00129	0.697
	STO CombMNZ	0.210	0.00244	0.693
	MinMax CombMNZ	0.199	0.00243	**0.704**

Table 8: System combination over all three teams. CombMNZ produces the best result for both text and speech. In the case of text, we attained a 5 point absolute increase (from 0.65 to 0.70), and in speech a 9 point absolute increase (from 0.61 to 0.70) over the single best system. P_{miss} and P_{FA} is the probability of misses and false alarm, respectively.

For COMBMNZ, to investigate the effect of normalization before the combination, we implement two normalization approaches: (1) MINMAX: a standard score normalization technique (Lee, 1997): $s'_m = \frac{s_m - \min S_m}{\max S_m - \min S_m}$, where s_m is the retrieved score from a system $m \in M$, set of all systems, and S_m is the set of all scores from the system m, and (2) STO: a sum-to-one normalization technique (Karakos et al., 2013), where s'_m is the original score divided by the sum of the scores for all returned document scores for a particular query (down to some fixed per-system threshold).

After normalization, CombMNZ is applied as followed:

$$CombMNZ = t \cdot \sum_{m=1}^{M} s'_m \tag{1}$$

where t is the number of times the document is retrieved across the $|M|$ systems.

After the CombMNZ combination, we apply a query-specific rank cutoff based on averaging the number of returned documents of the three teams per each query. A cutoff is essential for the system combination if we want to achieve a competitive AQWV: without the cutoff, CombMNZ will have the same AQWV as the union of the result sets over the three teams.

For both speech and text, all combination methods significantly outperform the single systems by a notable margin[3]. For text, the MINMAX COMBMNZ method outperforms all other combination methods significantly. For speech, MINMAX COMBMNZ achieves the best result, though it is not significantly better than the other combination methods.

Comparing COMBMNZ and MAJORITY VOTE, the overall difference on AQWV is relatively small. While COMBMNZ approaches are effective in reducing P_{miss}, the MAJORITY VOTE is effective in reducing P_{false_alarm}. This is in line with our intuition, as MAJORITY VOTE requires at least two teams to agree to retrieve the document, leading to a lower false alarm rate with a price of increased miss rate. COMBMNZ, on the other hand, combines a score-based combination approach ($\sum_{m=1}^{M} s'_m$) with a voting approach (t), which often leads to better ranking. This, together with a reasonable cutoff, helps to reduce the misses without raising the false alarm rate too much.

5. Conclusion and Future Work

One hallmark of the MATERIAL program is a focus on rapid system development, through the so-called "surprise language exercises". The detailed system results that we have started to analyze in this paper were released just over a week before this workshop's submission deadline, so we

---

[3]Statistically significant at $p < 0.05$, two-sided paired t-test.

might think of these results as having been from something of a "surprise analysis exercise". Despite the short time, we've been able to see four interesting phenomena that may help to guide future work. Perhaps most interestingly, we have identified a document length effect, with systems tending to rank longer text documents earlier, and longer speech recordings later, in a ranked list (i.e., closer to the decision threshold). We also noted that missed relevant documents tended, on average, to be shorter than correctly found relevant documents for two of the three teams. Together, these observations suggest that additional length normalization could pay off. We have also seen that mapping from query terms to document content (at least in text, the condition we were able to analyze) poses a number of systematic challenges, each of which is amenable to further research. Our analysis of system behavior in the zero-relevant case, when there are no relevant documents to be found for some queries, indicates that better modeling that condition could yield useful improvements, at least as measured by the program's target measure (AQWV). This last point is potentially of substantial interest well beyond MATERIAL because zero-relevant cases are common in many applications of search technology, and that is not a condition for which present retrieval systems are typically optimized. Finally, its been said that quantity has a quality all its own, and our results again show that to be true for system combination. Although voting is a straightforward approach to merging results from multiple set-based retrieval systems, we have found that, as would be expected, some additional gain can be achieved when confidence scores are available.

We are nowhere near exhausting the potential of this sort of analysis. For one thing, we have comparably large test collections available in two other languages, Swahili and Somali, and we might thus consider exchanging system results on such collections in the future. Such analysis might be particularly useful for Somali, which has proven to be a particularly challenging language. One limitation of our present approach, relying as it does on submitted result sets, is that it is one-sided—we can analyze confidence scores for items that were returned, but not for those that weren't. In a future study, it might prove productive to look at the other side of the decision boundary as well. There is also surely much to be learned from looking at what each individual team did relatively well at and trying to associate that with specifics of that team's system design, a question that was beyond the scope of this first analysis of ours. So we still do have miles to go before we sleep (Monteiro, 2010), but we believe that these first steps at document-scale analysis of results from multiple systems offer some useful insight into the current state of the art, and that they point the way toward future analyses of this type.

6. Acknowledgments

This research has been supported by the Office of the Director of National Intelligence (ODNI), Intelligence Advanced Research Projects Activity (IARPA), via contract FA8650-17-C-9117. The views and conclusions contained herein are those of the authors and should not be interpreted as necessarily representing the official policies, either expressed or implied, of ODNI, IARPA, or the U.S. Government. The U.S. Government is authorized to reproduce and distribute reprints for governmental purposes notwithstanding any copyright annotation therein. This work was also supported by a gift of Google Cloud Platform research credits.

7. Bibliographical References

Boschee, E., Barry, J., Billa, J., Freedman, M., et al. (2019). SARAL: A Low-Resource Cross-Lingual Domain-Focused Information Retrieval System for Effective Rapid Document Triage. In *ACL*.

Cooper, W. (1971). A definition of relevance for information retrieval. *Information Storage and Retrieval*, 7(1):19 – 37.

Gonzalo, J. and Oard, D. W. (2004). iCLEF 2004 track overview: pilot experiments in interactive cross-language question answering. In *CLEF*.

Karakos, D., Schwartz, R., Tsakalidis, S., Zhang, L., Ranjan, S., et al. (2013). Score normalization and system combination for improved keyword spotting. In *ASRU*.

Lee, J. H. (1997). Analyses of multiple evidence combination. In *SIGIR*.

Metzler, D. and Croft, W. B. (2005). A Markov random field model for term dependencies. In *SIGIR*.

Monteiro, G. (2010). Life of a Poem "Stopping by Woods on a Snowy Evening". *The Robert Frost Review*.

Nie, J.-Y. (2010). Cross-language information retrieval. *Synthesis Lectures on Human Language Technologies*.

NIST. (2016). Evaluation Plan for the IARPA MATERIAL Program. https://www.nist.gov/system/files/documents/ 2019/10/16/material_op1_eval_plan_v0.0.9.pdf.

Oard, D. W. and Diekema, A. R. (1998). Cross-language information retrieval. *Annual Review of Information Science and Technology (ARIST)*.

Oard, D. W., Carpuat, M., Galuščáková, P., Barrow, J., Nair, S., Niu, X., Shing, H.-C., et al. (2019). Surprise Languages: Rapid-Response Cross-Language IR. In *EVIA*.

Rubino, C. (2016). IARPA MATERIAL program. https://www.iarpa.gov/index.php/research-programs/ material/material-baa.

Shaw, J. and Fox, E. (1994). Combination of multiple searches. In *TREC*.

Shing, H.-C., Barrow, J., Galuščáková, P., Oard, D., and Resnik, P. (2019). Unsupervised system combination for set-based retrieval with expectation maximization. In *CLEF*.

Zavorin, I., Bills, A., Corey, C., Morrison, M., Tong, A., and Tong, R. (2020). Corpora for Cross-Language Information Retrieval in Six Less-Resourced Languages. In *LREC 2020 Workshop on Cross-Language Search and Summarization of Text and Speech*.

Zbib, R., Zhao, L., Karakos, D., Hartmann, W., DeYoung, J., , et al. (2019). Neural-network lexical translation for cross-lingual IR from text and speech. In *SIGIR*.

Zhao, L., Zbib, R., Jiang, Z., Karakos, D., and Huang, Z. (2019). Weakly Supervised Attentional Model for Low Resource Ad-hoc Cross-lingual Information Retrieval. In *Proceedings of the 2nd Workshop on Deep Learning Approaches for Low-Resource NLP (DeepLo)*.

Proceedings of the Cross-Language Search and Summarization of Text and Speech Workshop, pages 22–25
Language Resources and Evaluation Conference (LREC 2020), Marseille, 11–16 May 2020
© European Language Resources Association (ELRA), licensed under CC-BY-NC

SEARCHER: Shared Embedding Architecture for Effective Retrieval

Joel Barry, Elizabeth Boschee, Marjorie Freedman, Scott Miller
Information Sciences Institute, University of Southern California
{joelb, boschee, mrf, smiller}@isi.edu

Abstract

We describe an approach to cross lingual information retrieval that does not rely on explicit translation of either document or query terms. Instead, both queries and documents are mapped into a shared embedding space where retrieval is performed. We discuss potential advantages of the approach in handling polysemy and synonymy. We present a method for training the model, and give details of the model implementation. We present experimental results for two cases: Somali-English and Bulgarian-English CLIR.

Keywords: CLIR, cross-lingual embeddings

1. Introduction

A fundamental design decision in cross-lingual information retrieval is whether to translate the queries, the documents, or both. In this paper, we discuss a substantially different alternative where neither the query nor the document is translated. Instead, both the queries and documents are projected into a shared embedding space and retrieval is performed there. The approach offers potential advantages in handling synonymy, i.e. where synonymous query terms can match a single document term (or vice-versa), as well as for document-language polysemy, i.e. where a particular document term can have one of several meanings depending on context. In tests on two languages, Somali and Bulgarian, we observed a level of performance that is competitive with the "document translation" approach, including when translation is performed using a state-of-the-art tensor-to-tensor model. For one of the languages, Somali, the shared embedding approach was also able to outperform a hybrid strategy involving both query and document translation. All experimental results were from IARPA's MATERIAL evaluation task.

2. Initial Experiments

Methods for constructing cross-lingual (and multilingual) word embeddings have been extensively investigated for the past several years (Hermann and Blunsom, 2014; Luong, Pham, and Manning, 2015; Gouws, Bengio, and Corrado, 2015) and several pre-trained resources are publicly available. To begin exploring the possibility of applying shared embeddings for CLIR, we constructed a baseline system and tested a few state-of-the-art publicly-available variants, including MUSE (Conneau et al., 2017). The baseline system architecture is shown in Figure 1.

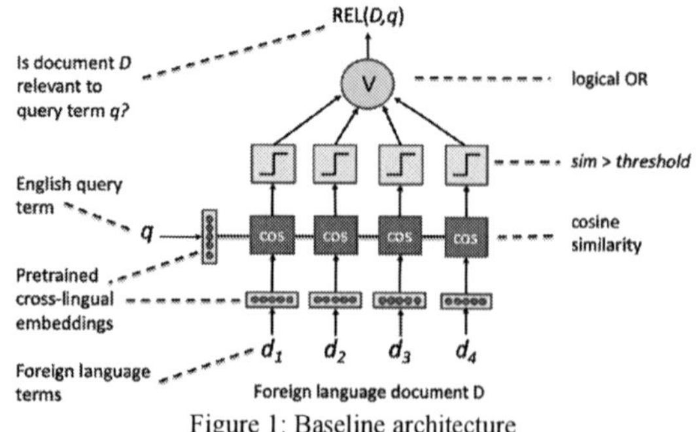

Figure 1: Baseline architecture

In this system, document relevancy is determined based on cosine distance between query and document terms. More specifically, a document is considered responsive to a query if at least one of the document words is within a fixed threshold (in embedding space) of the query. Despite basing our experiments on state-of-the-art embeddings, initial performance was low. The AQWV score (Actual Query Weighted Value) for MATERIAL's Swahili-English analysis set was 0.03; for Tagalog-English it was 0.07.

2.1 Limitations of the Baseline Approach

Three factors seemed to account for the low AQWV scores. First, embedding spaces are not uniform; some regions are densely packed with words while other regions are only sparsely populated. Thus, no consistent interpretation of distance exists, making the selection of a single matching threshold problematic. Second, although simple linear transformations are capable of aligning semantically-related words across languages, the alignments are not sufficiently precise to identify exact term translations – particularly for MATERIAL's lexical queries. Finally, our retrieval mechanism was massively under-parameterized; initial experiments attempted to optimize a complex CLIR task by adjusting only a single scalar threshold parameter.

3. Training Data and Objective Function

Overcoming these limitations would require a sufficiently parameterized model that could be trained for the CLIR task. Implicit in this approach is the need for training data and for a well-defined training objective. In principle, data provided by the MATERIAL program could provide the training examples and AQWV could serve as the objective function. However, MATERIAL's rules explicitly prohibit directly training on this data and, in any case, the relatively small number of queries and relevance judgements is insufficient to train an adequate model (e.g., embedding parameters alone require estimating millions of floating-point values).

Instead, we defined a simplified sentence-retrieval task for which training data is readily available. Specifically, given an English query term (q) and a foreign language sentence (S):

- **Sentence S is relevant to query q if there exists at least one plausible translation of S containing q.**

For this proxy task, large numbers of training examples can be extracted from a parallel corpus such as used to train machine translation systems. Specifically, any English term that occurs anywhere in a bitext sentence can be treated as a query and its corresponding foreign-language sentence treated as a positive example. Negative examples can be randomly drawn from foreign-language bitext sentences (any randomly selected sentence is probably not relevant, but we can additionally verify that its corresponding English sentence does not contain the query term).

Query	Sentence	Relevant
vehicle	Kifungu cha 50 cha kulipita gari jingine vibaya adhabu yake ni Sh. 400.	YES
vehicle	Alimweleza kama mgombea mfisadi zaidi kuwahi kuwania urais nchini Marekani.	NO
phones	Fikiria watu wa simu kwani Tanzania watu wengi wanatumia simu.	YES
phones	Sasa ni Msaidizi wa Ray Wilkins kwenye Timu ya Taifa ya Jordan.	NO

Figure 2: Examples of training instances

Figure 2 shows examples of training instances from a Swahili/English parallel corpus. The sentence in the first row translates to "The fine for passing another vehicle improperly is 400 shillings." Similarly, the sentence in the third row translates to "Think about people with phones since in Tanzania so many people are using phones." The sentences in rows 2 and 4 are randomly selected Swahili sentences that do not contain the query term.

Given a training corpus of such examples, the probability that a sentence S is relevant to a query q, i.e. $P(rel|S, q)$, can be optimized using the standard cross-entropy objective function H

$$H(X) = \sum_X z * -\log\left(p(rel|S, q) + (1 - z)\right.$$
$$\left. * -\log\left(1 - p(rel|S, q)\right)\right)$$

where X is the set of training examples and z are the true labels (1 for relevant, 0 for irrelevant).

For the actual MATERIAL task, the relevance of a document to a query phrase is taken as the maximum relevance over sentences in the document.

4. Model Architecture

Now that we have identified suitable training data and an objective function, we next consider the challenge of model design.

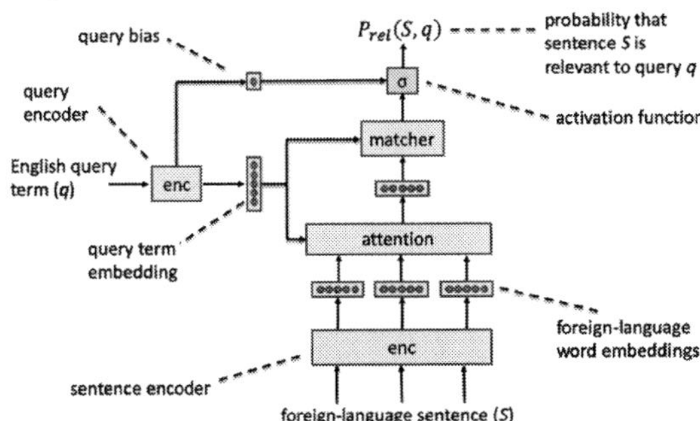

Figure 3, Generic SEARCHER Architecture

Here we introduce the following elements:

- Query encoder: maps English terms into the shared embedding space
- Sentence encoder: maps foreign-language terms into the shared embedding space

- Attention mechanism: selects regions of the sentence based on the query
- Matching mechanism: determines how closely the selected region matches the query
- Activation function: maps matching scores to probability values

An overview of the generic SEARCHER architecture is shown in Figure 3. The retrieval process proceeds as follows. First, each foreign-language word is mapped into the shared embedding space. These embeddings are contextualized, as described in Sections 5 and 6. Next, the English query term is mapped into the common embedding space. An attention mechanism then selects the region of the foreign-language sentence that appears most relevant to the query and outputs its embedding. The selected region's embedding is compared to the query by a matching function which outputs a matching score. Finally, the matching score is passed through an activation function that produces the probability of relevance. Importantly, this activation function also receives a separate query-specific bias value. This bias value helps overcome non-uniformity in the embedding space by requiring some terms to match more closely than others depending on the density of their surrounding neighborhoods. In all of our experiments, we use a sigmoidal activation function.

5. Contextualized Embedding Spaces

Beginning with models such as BERT (Devlin et al., 2018) and ELMO (Peters et al., 2018), contextualized embeddings have proven useful for a wide range of tasks. While MATERIAL's queries typically contain only one or a few words, and therefore offer little opportunity for query contextualization, our proxy CLIR task evaluates relevance over complete sentences, offering the possibility of contextualizing document embeddings. A potential advantage of such contextualization is the resolution of polysemous terms. Specifically, a contextualized model can learn to situate polysemous terms in different regions of the embedding space depending on context. For example the Swahili term "nyanya" can be translated alternatively as "grandmother" or "tomatoes," as shown in Figure 4. Ideally, a contextualized model will place the different senses of a polysemous term in different locations in the embedding space, thereby reducing the possibility of spurious matches (e.g. retrieving grandmothers when searching for tomatoes).

We note that in SEARCHER, contextualized embeddings are used only for document terms; non-contextual embeddings are used for query terms.

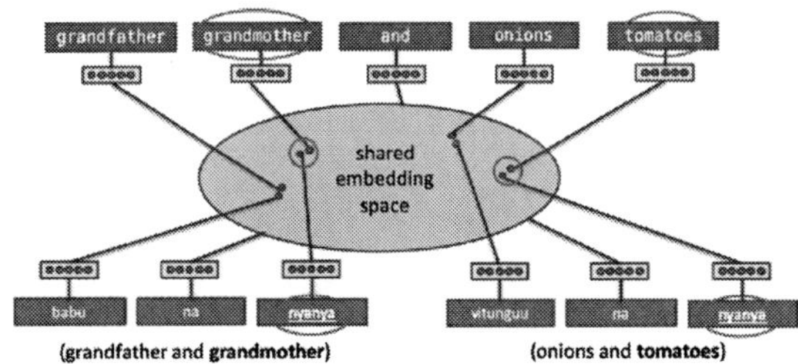

Figure 4: Polysemy in shared embedding space

Performing retrieval in a shared embedding space is also potentially useful for resolving synonymous terms. For example, the Swahili term 'gari' can be translated equivalently as "car" or "vehicle," as shown in Figure 5. Ideally, the model will place synonymous terms in similar positions in the embedding space, thereby increasing the possibility of matching any of the alternatives (e.g. retrieving a document containing "gari" whether the query term is "car" or "vehicle").

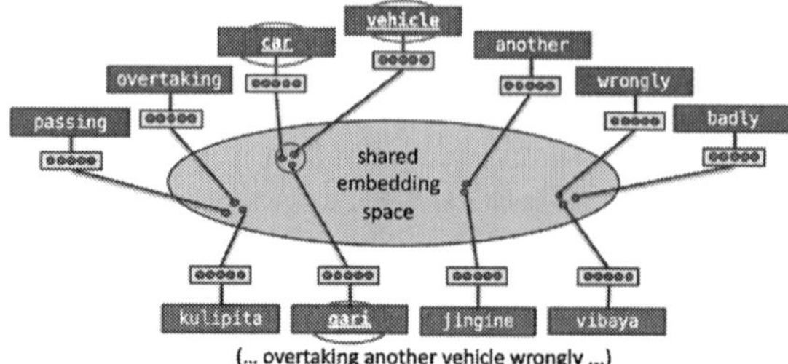

Figure 5: Synonymy in shared embedding space

6. Convolutional Encoder

In this section, we consider details of the sentence encoder mentioned in Section 4. Specifically, SEARCHER's sentence encoder produces contextualized embeddings using a deep convolutional model consisting of 15 convolution layers, each of diameter 3. This architecture yields a receptive field of 31 words, providing 15 words of context on each side of a term. The encoder is similar to that described in (Gehring et al., 2018).

In detail, each convolution block consists of a dropout layer, a convolution layer, a GLU layer (gated linear units), and residual connections. A fixed embedding size of 512 is maintained throughout the network.

We use an identical encoder in our convolutional machine translation system. In fact, we have found that pretraining the encoder in an MT setting, then transferring the encoder to SEARCHER, and continuing to train the remaining CLIR elements is an effective method for speeding convergence.

7. Simplifications

Our generic SEARCHER architecture leaves room for various alternatives at the level of individual components. For instance, while we use a convolutional sentence encoder, it would be perfectly reasonable to substitute a transformer architecture.

One alternative involving the attention and matching mechanisms leads to a particularly attractive simplification. Specifically, if the attention mechanism is the commonly used form:

$$ATT(S, q) = \sum_{i \in |S|} \alpha_i s_i$$

$$\alpha_i = \frac{\exp(e_i)}{\sum_{i \in |S|} \exp(e_i)}$$

$$e_i = q \cdot s_i$$

and the matcher is a simple dot product, then the resulting architecture (after some algebra) reduces to that shown in Figure 6.

We have found this simplified architecture to be effective, producing results at least as good as more complex variations. A further simplification is obtainable by replacing the softmax pooling layer with a hard max-pooling layer. Both simplified variations produce similar results. The softmax variation requires fewer training cycles (because max-pooling updates just the single best-matching term on each training cycle, whereas softmax pooling updates all words in proportion to their distance from the query). On the other hand, max pooling appears to yield slightly sharper probability distributions.

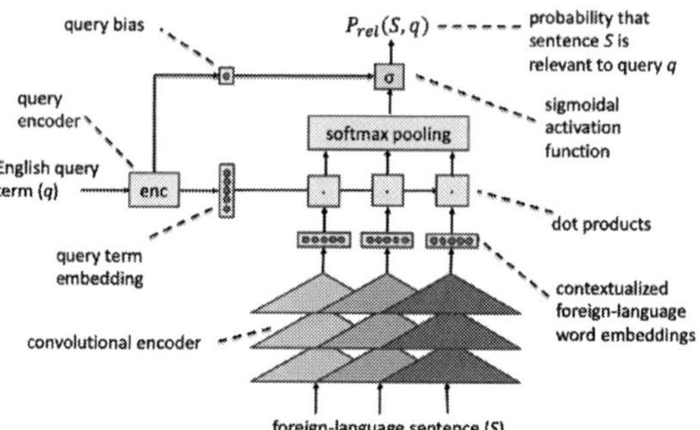

Figure 6: Simplified SEARCHER Architecture

8. Relation to the Baseline Model

The SEARCHER model shown in Figure 6 bears a striking resemblance to the baseline model described in Section 2. The most important difference is that the SEARCHER model is specifically trained to perform CLIR whereas the baseline model relies on pretrained embeddings. Other differences are:

- Contextualized embeddings replace individual word embeddings
- Dot products replace cosine distances (which are simply normalized dot products)
- Softmax pooling (essentially, a soft OR function) replaces the logical OR
- A sigmoidal activation function (essentially, a soft threshold) replaces hard thresholding
- The positions of the combining function (softmax/logical OR) and the activation function (sigmoid/hard threshold) are exchanged
- A bias term is introduced for each query term

9. Experimental Results

We tested SEARCHER in two MATERIAL languages, Somali and Bulgarian. For each language, we also evaluated traditional translation-based CLIR.

For the Somali case, we compare performance with several different machine translation models. These include syntax-based statistical machine translation and two types of neural machine translation: tensor-to-tensor (Vaswani et al., 2017) and convolutional (Gehring et al., 2018). For the neural models, we follow best practices in training, including the use of substantial back-translated data.

In all cases, the MT system is applied to translate the foreign language documents into English. We also evaluate alternatives where, in addition to translating the documents, we translate the English queries into the foreign language using translation tables obtained by a statistical alignment process. This strategy improves the probability of matching queries to documents by translating in both directions.

Results for Somali, as shown in Table 1, are encouraging. Entries in the table that are designated (+source) indicate the combined strategy where queries are also translated. Evaluating on two different MATERIAL data sets (designated analysis and dev), SEARCHER outperformed the "document translation" strategy for all translation models as well as the combined strategy where both the documents and the queries are translated.

System	AQWV analysis1/q1	AQWV dev1/q1
syntax-based MT	0.1537	0.2110
syntax-based MT + source	0.1643	0.2257
tensor-to-tensor MT	0.1753	0.1852
tensor-to-tensor + source	0.1904	0.2251
convolutional MT	0.1611	0.1965
convolutional MT + source	0.1814	0.2361
SEARCHER	**0.2290**	**0.2502**

Table 1: AQWV of various systems on Somali

For the Bulgarian case, we compare SEARCHER with only our best machine translation model, a tensor-to-tensor model, and evaluate only on MATERIAL analysis documents. Once again, the MT system is applied to translate the foreign-language documents into English. As before, we also evaluate the combined strategy, translating both documents and queries.

Results for Bulgarian are shown in Table 2. In this case, results are somewhat different. In general, performance is much better. SEARCHER's performance matches the "document translation" strategy alone. However, when query translation is added, the combined translation strategy noticeably outperforms SEARCHER. We suspect that part of the explanation for the differences in relative performance is the amount of training data available. Specifically, large quantities of paracrawl data for Bulgarian provide a significant boost in MT accuracy.

System	AQWV analysis1/q1
tensor-to-tensor MT	0.6527
tensor-to-tensor + source	0.6998
SEARCHER	0.6546

Table 2: AQWV for Bulgarian

10. Summary

We have conducted numerous experiments with SEARCHER models. We have identified an effective general architecture and derived simplified variations that perform well. We found that training for a proxy task (sentence retrieval) is a useful strategy and that adequate training examples can be derived from bitexts. While much work remains to be done, we have demonstrated that shared embedding space models can be an effective method for CLIR, providing a competitive alternative to document translation models, including those based on state-of-the-art neural MT. In one language, Somali, we found that SEARCHER outperformed all the translation-based alternatives that we evaluated.

11. Acknowledgements

This research is based upon work supported in part by the Office of the Director of National Intelligence (ODNI), Intelligence Advanced Research Projects Activity (IARPA), via contract # FA8650-17-C9116. The views and conclusions contained herein are those of the authors and should not be interpreted as necessarily representing the official policies, either expressed or implied, of ODNI, IARPA, or the U.S. Government. The U.S. Government is authorized to reproduce and distribute reprints for governmental purposes notwithstanding any copyright annotation therein.

12. References

Alexis Conneau, Guillaume Lample, Marc'Aurelio Ranzato, Ludovic Denoyer, Hervé Jégou, (2017). Word Translation Without Parallel Data, arXiv:1710.04087

Jacob Devlin, Ming-Wei Chang, Kenton Lee, Kristina Toutanova, (2018). BERT: Pre-training of Deep Bidirectional Transformers for Language Understanding, arXiv:1810.04805

Jonas Gehring, Michael Auli, David Grangier, Denis Yarats, Yann N. Dauphin, (2017). Convolutional Sequence to Sequence Learning, arXiv:1705.03122

Stephan Gouws, Yoshua Bengio, and Greg Corrado, (2015). Bilbowa: Fast bilingual distributed representations without word alignments. In Proc. of ICML

Thang Luong, Hieu Pham, and Christopher D. Manning, (2015). Bilingual word representations with monolingual quality in mind. In Proc. of the Workshop on Vector Space Modeling for NLP.

Karl Moritz Hermann and Phil Blunsom, (2014). Multilingual Models for Compositional Distributional Semantics. In Proc. of ACL.

Matthew E. Peters, Mark Neumann, Mohit Iyyer, Matt Gardner, Christopher Clark, Kenton Lee, Luke Zettlemoyer, (2018). Deep contextualized word representations, arXiv:1802.05365

Ashish Vaswani, Noam Shazeer, Niki Parmar, Jakob Uszkoreit, Llion Jones, Aidan N. Gomez, Lukasz Kaiser, Illia Polosukhin, (2017). Attention Is All You Need, arXiv:1706.03762

Proceedings of the Cross-Language Search and Summarization of Text and Speech Workshop, pages 26–31
Language Resources and Evaluation Conference (LREC 2020), Marseille, 11–16 May 2020
© European Language Resources Association (ELRA), licensed under CC-BY-NC

Cross-lingual Information Retrieval with BERT

Zhuolin Jiang[†], Amro El-Jaroudi[††], William Hartmann[†], Damianos Karakos[†], Lingjun Zhao[†]

[†]Raytheon BBN Technologies, Cambridge, MA, 02138
[‡]University of Pittsburgh, Pittsburgh, PA, 15261
{zhuolin.jiang, amro.a.eljaroudi-nr, william.hartmann, damianos.karakos, lingjun.zhao}@raytheon.com

Abstract

Multiple neural language models have been developed recently, *e.g.*, BERT and XLNet, and achieved impressive results in various NLP tasks including sentence classification, question answering and document ranking. In this paper, we explore the use of the popular bidirectional language model, BERT, to model and learn the relevance between English queries and foreign-language documents in the task of cross-lingual information retrieval. A deep relevance matching model based on BERT is introduced and trained by finetuning a pretrained multilingual BERT model with weak supervision, using home-made CLIR training data derived from parallel corpora. Experimental results of the retrieval of Lithuanian documents against short English queries show that our model is effective and outperforms the competitive baseline approaches.

Keywords: Cross-lingual Information Retrieval; Neural Network Models; Relevance Matching; Weak Supervision

1. Introduction

A traditional cross-lingual information retrieval (CLIR) system consists of two components: machine translation and monolingual information retrieval (Nie, 2010). The idea is to solve the translation problem first, then the cross-lingual IR problem become monolingual IR. However, the performance of translation-based approaches is limited by the quality of the machine translation and it needs to handle to translation ambiguity (Zhou et al., 2012). One possible solution is to consider the translation alternatives of individual words of queries or documents as in (Zbib et al., 2019; Xu and Weischedel, 2000), which provides more possibilities for matching query words in relevant documents compared to using single translations. But the alignment information is necessarily required in the training stage of the CLIR system to extract target-source word pairs from parallel data and this is not a trivial task.

To achieve good performance in IR, deep neural networks have been widely used in this task. These approaches can be roughly divided into two categories. The first class of approaches uses pretrained word representations or embeddings, such as word2vec (Mikolov et al., 2013) and GloVe (Pennington et al., 2014), directly to improve IR models. Usually these word embeddings are pretrained on large scale text corpora using co-occurrence statistics, so they have modeled the underlying data distribution implicitly and should be helpful for building discriminative models. (Vulic and Moens, 2015) and (Litschko et al., 2018) used pretrained bilingual embeddings to represent queries and foreign documents, and then ranked documents by cosine similarity. (Zheng and Callan, 2015) used word2vec embeddings to learn query term weights. However, their training objectives of trained neural embeddings are different from the objective of IR.

The second set of approaches design and train deep neural networks based on IR objectives. These methods have shown impressive results on monolingual IR datasets (Xiong et al., 2017; Guo et al., 2016; Dehghani et al., 2017). They usually rely on large amounts of query-document relevance annotated data that are expensive to obtain, especially for low-resource language pairs in cross-lingual IR tasks. Moreover, it is not clear whether they generalize well when documents and queries are in different languages.

Recently multiple pretrained language models have been developed such as BERT (Devlin et al., 2019) and XLNet (Yang et al., 2019), that model the underlying data distribution and learn the linguistic patterns or features in language. These models have outperformed traditional word embeddings on various NLP tasks (Yang et al., 2019; Devlin et al., 2019; Peters et al., 2018; Lan et al., 2019). These pretrained models also provided new opportunities for IR. Therefore, several recent works have successfully applied BERT pretrained models for monolingual IR (Dai and Callan, 2019; Akkalyoncu Yilmaz et al., 2019) and passage re-ranking (Nogueira and Cho, 2019).

In this paper, we extend and apply BERT as a ranker for CLIR. We introduce a cross-lingual deep relevance matching model for CLIR based on BERT. We finetune a pretrained multilingual model with home-made CLIR data and obtain very promising results. In order to finetune the model, we construct a large amount of training data from parallel data, which is mainly used for machine translation and is much easier to obtain compared to the relevance labels of query-document pairs. In addition, we don't require the source-target alignment information to construct training samples and avoid the quality issues of machine translation in traditional CLIR. The entire model is specifically optimized using a CLIR objective. Our main contributions are:

- We introduce a cross-lingual deep relevance architecture with BERT, where a pretrained multilingual BERT model is adapted for cross-lingual IR.

- We define a proxy CLIR task which can be used to easily construct CLIR training data from bitext data, without requiring any amount of relevance labels of query-document pairs in different languages.

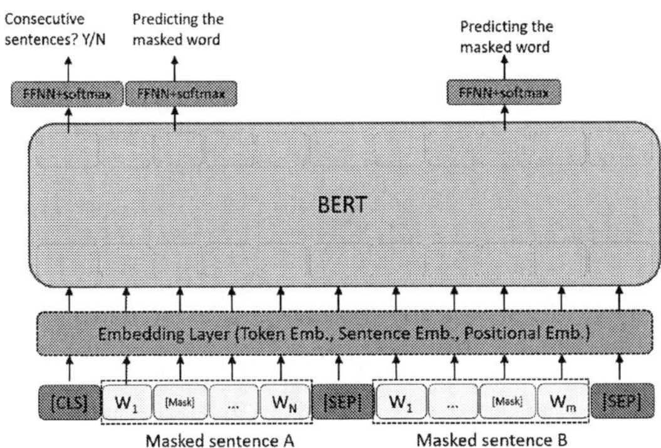

Figure 1: BERT pretraining architecture (Devlin et al., 2019). FFNN denotes feed-forward neural network.

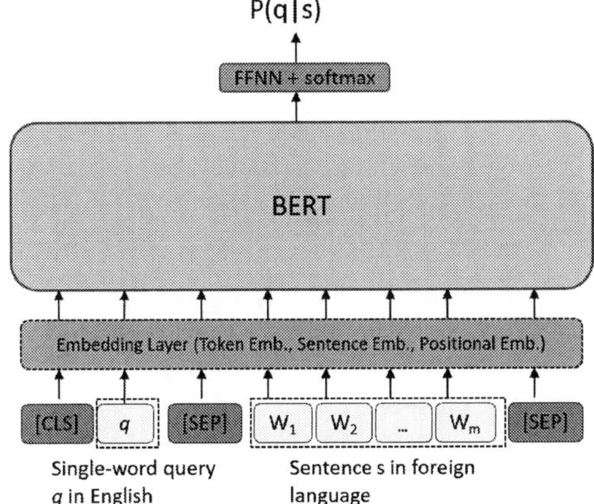

Figure 2: Fine-tuned CLIR BERT model architecture.

2. Our approach

2.1. Motivation

BERT (Devlin et al., 2019) is the first bidirectional language model, which makes use of left and right word contexts simultaneously to predict word tokens. It is trained by optimizing two objectives: masked word prediction and next sentence prediction. As shown in Figure 1, the inputs are a pair of masked sentences in the same language, where some tokens in the both sentences are replaced by symbol '[Mask]'. The BERT model is trained to predict these masked tokens, by capturing within or across sentence meaning (or context), which is important for IR. The second objective aims to judge whether the sentences are consecutive or not. It encourages the BERT model to model the relationship between two sentences. The self-attention mechanism in BERT models the local interactions of words in sentence A with words in sentence B, so it can learn pairwise sentence or word-token relevance patterns. The entire BERT model is pretrained on large scale text corpora and learns linguistic patterns in language. So search tasks with little training data can still benefit from the pretrained model.

Finetuning BERT on search task makes it learn IR specific features. It can capture query-document exact term matching, bi-gram features for monolingual IR as introduced in (Dai and Callan, 2019). Local matchings of words and n-grams have proven to be strong neural IR features. Bigram modeling is important, because it can learn the meaning of word compounds (bi-grams) from the meanings of individual words. Motivated by this work, we aim to finetune the pretrained BERT model for cross-lingual IR.

2.2. Finetuning BERT for CLIR

Figure 2 shows the proposed CLIR model architecture with BERT. The inputs are pairs of single-word queries q in English and foreign-language sentences s. This is different from the pretraining model in Figure 1, where the model is fed with pairs of sentences in the same language. We concatenate the query q and the foreign-language sentence s into a text sequence '[[CLS], q, [SEP], s, [SEP]]'. The output embedding of the first token '[CLS]' is used as a representation of the entire query-sentence pair. Then it is fed into a single layer feed-forward neural network to pre-

dict the relevance score, which is the probability, $p(q|s)$, of query q occurring in sentence s.

There are three types of parameterized layers in this model: (1) an embedding layer including token embedding, sentence embedding and positional embedding (Devlin et al., 2019); (2) BERT layers which are 12 layers of transformer blocks; (3) a feed-forward neural network (FFNN) which is a single layer neural network in our implementation. The embedding layer and BERT layer are initialized with the pretrained BERT model [1], while the FFNN is learned from scratch. During finetuning, the entire model is tuned to learn more CLIR-specific features. We only train the model using single-word queries since the queries in MATERIAL dataset are typically short and keyword based, but our approach can be easily extended to be multi-word queries or query phrases. After finetuning, this model produces a sentence-level relevance score for a pair of input query and foreign language sentence.

For the CLIR task, given a user-issued query Q, the foreign-language document Doc is ranked by its relevance score with respect to Q. The document-level relevance score $P(Doc$ is $R|Q)$ is calculated by aggregating the sentence-level scores with a Noisy-OR model:

$$P(Doc \text{ is } R|Q) = P(Q \text{ occurs at least in one sentence in } Doc)$$
$$= 1 - \prod_{s \in Doc} (1 - P(Q|s)) \qquad (1)$$
$$= 1 - \prod_{s \in Doc} (1 - \prod_{q \in Q} p(q|s))$$

Note that a multi-word query will be split into multiple single-word queries when computing document-level relevance scores. The individual query terms $q \in Q$ are modeled independently.

---

[1] We used the pretrained multi-lingual BERT model, which is trained on the concatenation of monolingual Wikipedia corpora from 104 languages. It has 12 layers, 768 hidden dimensions, 12 self-attention heads and 110 million parameters.

Query in English	Foreign-language sentence	Relevant
doctors	medikų teigimu dabar veikianti sistema efektyvi	Yes
allege	medikų teigimu dabar veikianti sistema efektyvi	Yes
controller	medikų teigimu dabar veikianti sistema efektyvi	No
leisure	medikų teigimu dabar veikianti sistema efektyvi	No

Table 1: Four training examples derived from a bitext: *Source-Lithuanian*: medikų teigimu dabar veikianti sistema efektyvi; *Target-English*: <u>doctors</u> <u>allege</u> that the system currently in operation is effective.

2.3. Finetuning using Weak Supervision

To finetune the BERT CLIR model, we start with bitext data in English and the desired foreign-language. We then define a proxy CLIR task to construct training samples: Given a foreign-language sentence s and an English query term q, sentence s is relevant to q if q occurs in one plausible translation of s. Any non-stop English word in the bitext can serve as a single-word query. The English word and its the corresponding foreign-language sentence constitute a positive example. Similarly, we randomly select other words from the English vocabulary, which are not in the English sentence, to be query words to construct negative examples. Table 1 shows an illustration of constructing four training examples from a bitext in Lithuanian and English. We select 'doctors' and 'allege' in the English sentence as two single-word queries and use the Lithuanian sentence to construct two positive examples, and pick another two words "controller" and "leisure" in the English vocabulary, which are not in the English sentence, to construct negative examples. In this way, we can construct a large-scale training corpus for CLIR using parallel data only, which are much easier to obtain compared to query-document relevance annotated data.

3. Experiments

We report experimental results on the retrieval of Lithuanian text and speech documents against short English queries. We use queries and retrieval corpora provided by the IARPA MATERIAL program. The retrieval corpora have two datasets: an analysis set (about 800 documents) and a development set (about 400 documents). The query set $Q1$ contains 300 queries.

To construct the training set, we use parallel sentences released under the MATERIAL (MAT, 2017) and the LO-RILEI (LOR, 2015) programs. We also include a parallel lexicon downloaded from Panlex (Kamholz et al., 2014). These parallel data contain about 2.6 million pairs of bitexts. We extract about 54 million training samples from these parallel data to finetune BERT. The positive-negative ratio of CLIR training data is 1 : 2. To finetune BERT, we use the ADAM optimizer with an initial learning rate set to 1×10^{-5}, batch size of 32 and max sequence length of 128. We report the results from the model trained for one epoch. The training took one week using a Telsa V100 GPU.

We also extract 877K testing samples from the bitexts in MATERIAL Lithuanian analysis set to test the classification accuracy of different neural CLIR models. The positive-negative ratio of this test set is 1 : 1. In addition, we evaluate our model on the MATERIAL Lithuanian analysis set and development set in terms of Mean Average Precision (MAP) and Maximum Query Weighted Value (MQWV) scores. MQWV is used in the MATERIAL program and denotes the maximum of the metric Average Query Weighted Value (AQWV): $AQWV = 1 - P_{Miss} - \beta P_{FA}$, where P_{Miss} is the average per-query miss rate, P_{FA} is the average per-query false alarm rate and β is a constant that changes the relative importance of the two types of error. We use $\beta = 40$. AQWV is the score using a single selected detection threshold. MQWV is the score that could be obtained with the optimal detection threshold. To verify the effectiveness of our BERT CLIR model, we compare against four baselines:

Probabilistic CLIR Model (Xu and Weischedel, 2000) is a generative probabilistic model which requires a probabilistic translation dictionary. The translation dictionary is generated from the word alignments of the parallel data. We used the GIZA++ (Och and Ney, 2003) and the Berkeley aligner (Haghighi et al., 2009) to estimate lexical translation probabilities.

Probabilistic Occurrence Model (Zbib et al., 2019) computes the document relevance score as the probability that each query term q occurs at least once in the document. $P(Doc \text{ is } R|Q) = \prod_{q \in Q} \left[1 - \prod_{f \in Doc} (1 - p(q|f)) \right]$, where f is a foreign term in the document.

Query Relevance Attentional Neural Network Model (QRANN) (Zhao et al., 2019) uses an attention mechanism to compute a context vector derived from word embeddings in the foreign sentences, followed by a feed-forward layer to capture the relationship between query words. The idea is similar to a single transformer layer. The QRANN models are trained on multi-word queries, which are noun phrases in the English sentences of bitexts, and single-word queries.

Dot-product Model is a simplified version of QRANN, that computes a context vector from the word embeddings of foreign sentence using multiplicative attention, followed by the dot product of between the query embeddings and the context vector. The dot-product model is trained using single-word queries only.

3.1. Classification Accuracy of different neural CLIR models

The QRANN and Dot-product models are trained using the same CLIR training data used to train BERT model described earlier. The classification results of different neural CLIR approaches are shown in Table 2. The CLIR BERT model achieves the best result compared to other two neural models. From the confusion matrix in the table, BERT significantly improves the performance of classifying relevant query-sentence pairs (*i.e.*, true positives), while matching the performance of classifying irrelevant query-sentence

Approach	Accuracy	Confusion Matrix	
BERT	**95.3%**	0.93	0.07
		0.02	0.98
Dot-Product	84.2%	0.74	0.26
		0.07	0.93
QRANN	87.3%	0.73	0.27
		0.003	0.997

Table 2: Performance of classification accuracy on the generated query-sentence pairs from the bitexts of the MATERIAL analysis set. The first column in the confusion matrix corresponds to the positive class (*i.e.*, relevant query-sentence pair) while the second the column is the negative class.

Approach	phrase query subset	entire query set
Prob. CLIR	57.4	**61.2**
Prob. Occurrence	51.4	56.9
BERT	**61.3**	56.8
Dot-Product	50.8	39.2
QRANN	55.8	45.5

Table 3: Performance of MAP scores on the MATERIAL analysis set and Q1 queries.

pairs (*i.e.*, true negatives).

3.2. MAP scores of different CLIR models

We compare the MAP score of the BERT model with those of other CLIR models in Table 3. In the table, we report MAP scores on the phrase query subset and the entire query set separately, to see how our model trained with single-word queries performs on query phrases. In the model training stage, QRANN model is the only model that is trained with the query phrases directly, all other models (including BERT) in this experiment will split a multi-word query or query phrase into multiple single-word queries. Surprisingly, the BERT MAP scores for the phrase query subset is the best compared with the performances of other approaches. It shows that BERT model can produce better relevance model for single-word queries and foreign-language sentence.The table also shows that BERT outperforms the other neural approaches over the entire query set.

3.3. MQWV scores of different CLIR models

We compare BERT models with other CLIR models in terms of MQWV scores. The results are summarized in Table 4. The first row in the table shows the best results of non-neural CLIR models, which are probabilistic CLIR model and probabilistic occurrence model. In this table, we separate the results based on the type of source documents: text or speech. Speech documents are converted into text documents via automatic speech recognition (Povey et al., 2011). The results of the BERT model on the speech sets are the best, compared with the non-neural CLIR systems, QRANN and Dot-product models, while the results on the text sets are comparable to those from the non-neural systems, and better than the other neural systems.

Approach	Analysis Set		Development Set	
	Text	Speech	Text	Speech
Best non-neural system	**66.3**	63.3	**68.8**	64.0
BERT	65.7	**65.4**	61.8	**65.1**
Dot-Product	61.0	60.4	56.1	63.7
QRANN	62.3	58.4	57.2	65.0

Table 4: MQWV scores on the Lithuanian analysis and development sets and Q1 queries.

3.4. Analysis on attention patterns from BERT

In Figure 3, we visualize the attention patterns produced by the attention heads from a transformer layer for the input English query 'writing well' and the foreign-language sentence 'mano nuomone ši autore rašo arba gerai arba blogai arba vidutiniškai'. The query term 'writing' attends to the foreign word 'rašo' (source-target word matching), while also attends to the foreign word 'gerai' , which correspond to the next English word 'well' in the query (bigram modeling). BERT CLIR model is able to capture these local matching features, which have been proven to be strong neural IR features.

4. Conclusions

We introduce a deep relevance matching model based on BERT language modeling architecture for cross-lingual document retrieval. The self-attention based architecture models the interactions of query words with words in the foreign-language sentence. The relevance model is initialized by the pretrained multi-lingual BERT model, and then finetuned with home-made CLIR training data that are derived from parallel data. The results of the CLIR BERT model on the data released by the MATERIAL program are better than two other competitive neural baselines, and comparable to the results of the probabilistic CLIR model. Our future work will use public IR datasets in English to learn IR features with BERT and transfer them to cross-lingual IR.

Acknowledgement

This work was supported by the Intelligence Advanced Research Projects Activity (IARPA) via Department of Defense US Air Force Research Laboratory contract number FA8650-17-C-9118.

5. Bibliographical References

Akkalyoncu Yilmaz, Z., Wang, S., Yang, W., Zhang, H., and Lin, J. (2019). Applying BERT to document retrieval with birch. In *Proceedings of the 2019 EMNLP-IJCNLP*.

Dai, Z. and Callan, J. (2019). Deeper text understanding for ir with contextual neural language modeling. In *Proceedings of the 42nd International ACM SIGIR Conference on Research and Development in Information Retrieval*.

Dehghani, M., Zamani, H., Severyn, A., Kamps, J., and Croft, W. B. (2017). Neural ranking models with weak supervision. In *Proceedings of the 40th International*

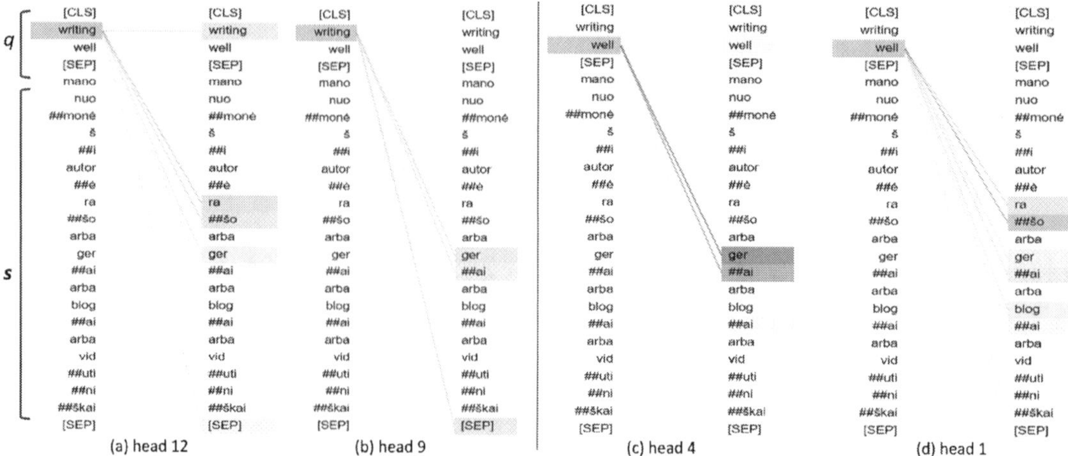

Figure 3: Visualization of CLIR BERT model. Colors identify the corresponding attention heads, while the line weight reflects the attention score. Different heads from layer 12 can capture different matching features. Word pieces' ra' , '##šo' in Lithuanian correspond to ''write' in English while 'ger', '##ai' are for 'well' in English. Head 12 and head 4 in (a)(c) can capture source-target word matching, head9 and head1 in (b)(d) could attend to its previous or next words (bigram modeling).

ACM SIGIR Conference on Research and Development in Information Retrieval.

Devlin, J., Chang, M.-W., Lee, K., and Toutanova, K. (2019). BERT: Pre-training of deep bidirectional transformers for language understanding. In *Proceedings of the 2019 Conference of the North American Chapter of the Association for Computational Linguistics: Human Language Technologies.*

Guo, J., Fan, Y., Ai, Q., and Croft, W. B. (2016). A deep relevance matching model for ad-hoc retrieval. In *Proceedings of the 25th ACM International on Conference on Information and Knowledge Management.*

Haghighi, A., Blitzer, J., DeNero, J., and Klein, D. (2009). Better word alignments with supervised itg models. In *Proceedings of the Joint Conference of the 47th Annual Meeting of the ACL and the 4th International Joint Conference on Natural Language Process.*

Kamholz, D., Pool, J., and Colowick, S. (2014). PanLex: Building a resource for panlingual lexical translation. In *Proceedings of the Ninth International Conference on Language Resources and Evaluation (LREC'14).*

Lan, Z.-Z., Chen, M., Goodman, S., Gimpel, K., Sharma, P., and Soricut, R. (2019). Albert: A lite bert for self-supervised learning of language representations. *ArXiv.*

Litschko, R., Glavas, G., Ponzetto, S. P., and Vulic, I. (2018). Unsupervised cross-lingual information retrieval using monolingual data only. In *Proceedings of the International ACM SIGIR Conference on Research and Development in Information Retrieval.*

(2015). Darpa lorelei program - broad agency announcement (baa). https://www.darpa.mil/program/low-resource-languages-for-emergent-incidents.

(2017). Iarpa material program - broad agency announcement (baa). https://www.iarpa.gov/index.php/research-programs/material.

Mikolov, T., Sutskever, I., Chen, K., Corrado, G. S., and Dean, J. (2013). Distributed representations of words and phrases and their compositionality. In *Advances in Neural Information Processing Systems.* Curran Associates, Inc.

Nie, J.-Y. (2010). *Cross-Language Information Retrieval.* Morgan and Claypool Publishers.

Nogueira, R. and Cho, K. (2019). Passage re-ranking with BERT. volume abs/1901.04085.

Och, F. J. and Ney, H. (2003). A systematic comparison of various statistical alignment models. *Computational Linguistics.*

Pennington, J., Socher, R., and Mannin, C. D. (2014). Glove: Global vectors for word representation. In *Empirical Methods in Natural Language Processing (EMNLP).*

Peters, M., Neumann, M., Iyyer, M., Gardner, M., Clark, C., Lee, K., and Zettlemoyer, L. (2018). Deep contextualized word representations. In *Proceedings of the 2018 Conference of the North American Chapter of the Association for Computational Linguistics: Human Language Technologies.*

Povey, D., Ghoshal, A., Boulianne, G., Burget, L., Glembek, O., Goel, N., Hannemann, M., Motlicek, P., Qian, Y., Schwarz, P., Silovsky, J., Stemmer, G., and Vesely, K. (2011). The kaldi speech recognition toolkit. In *IEEE 2011 Workshop on Automatic Speech Recognition and Understanding.*

Vulic, I. and Moens, M.-F. (2015). Monolingual and cross-lingual information retrieval models based on (bilingual) word embeddings. In *Proceedings of the 38th International ACM SIGIR Conference on Research and Development in Information Retrieval.*

Xiong, C., Dai, Z., Callan, J., Liu, Z., and Power, R. (2017). End-to-end neural ad-hoc ranking with kernel pooling. In *Proceedings of the 40th International ACM SIGIR Conference on Research and Development in Information Retrieval.*

Xu, J. and Weischedel, R. (2000). Cross-lingual information retrieval using hidden markov models. In *Proceedings of the 2000 Joint SIGDAT Conference on Empirical Methods in Natural Language Processing*.

Yang, Z., Dai, Z., Yang, Y., Carbonell, J., Salakhutdinov, R. R., and Le, Q. V. (2019). Xlnet: Generalized autoregressive pretraining for language understanding. In *Advances in Neural Information Processing Systems 32*.

Zbib, R., Zhao, L., Karakos, D., Hartmann, W., DeYoung, J., Huang, Z., Jiang, Z., Rivkin, N., Zhang, L., Schwartz, R. M., and Makhoul, J. (2019). Neural-network lexical translation for cross-lingual IR from text and speech. In *Proceedings of the 42nd International ACM SIGIR Conference on Research and Development in Information Retrieval*.

Zhao, L., Zbib, R., Jiang, Z., Karakos, D., and Huang, Z. (2019). Weakly supervised attentional model for low resource ad-hoc cross-lingual information retrieval. In *Proceedings of the 2nd Workshop on Deep Learning Approaches for Low-Resource NLP (DeepLo 2019)*.

Zheng, G. and Callan, J. (2015). Learning to reweight terms with distributed representations. In *Proceedings of the 38th International ACM SIGIR Conference on Research and Development in Information Retrieval*.

Zhou, D., Truran, M., Brailsford, T., Wade, V., and Ashman, H. (2012). Translation techniques in cross-language information retrieval. *ACM Comput. Surv.*, 45(1):1–44.

Proceedings of the Cross-Language Search and Summarization of Text and Speech Workshop, pages 32–37
Language Resources and Evaluation Conference (LREC 2020), Marseille, 11–16 May 2020
© European Language Resources Association (ELRA), licensed under CC-BY-NC

A Comparison of Unsupervised Methods for
Ad hoc Cross-Lingual Document Retrieval

Elaine Zosa, Mark Granroth-Wilding, Lidia Pivovarova
University of Helsinki
Helsinki, Finland
firstname.lastname@helsinki.fi

Abstract

We address the problem of linking related documents across languages in a multilingual collection. We evaluate three diverse unsupervised methods to represent and compare documents: (1) multilingual topic model; (2) cross-lingual document embeddings; and (3) Wasserstein distance. We test the performance of these methods in retrieving news articles in Swedish that are known to be related to a given Finnish article. The results show that ensembles of the methods outperform the stand-alone methods, suggesting that they capture complementary characteristics of the documents.

1. Introduction

We address the problem of retrieving related documents across languages through unsupervised cross-lingual methods that do not use translations or other lexical resources, such as dictionaries. There is a multitude of multilingual resources on the Internet such as Wikipedia, multilingual news sites, and historical archives. Many users may speak multiple languages or work in a context where discovering related documents in different languages is valuable, such as historical enquiry. This calls for tools that relate resources across language boundaries.

We choose to focus on methods that do not use translations because lexical resources and translation models vary across languages and time periods. Our goal is to find methods that are applicable across these contexts without extensive fine-tuning or manual annotation. Much work on cross-lingual document retrieval (CLDR) has focused on *cross-lingual word embeddings* but topic-based methods have also been used (Wang et al., 2016). Previous work has applied such cross-lingual learning methods to *known item search* where the task is to retrieve one relevant document given a query document (Balikas et al., 2018; Josifoski et al., 2019; Litschko et al., 2019). We are interested in *ad hoc retrieval* where there could be any number of relevant documents and the task is to rank the documents in the target collection according to their relevance to the query document (Voorhees, 2003).

Here we evaluate three existing unsupervised or weakly supervised methods previously used in CLDR for slightly different tasks: (1) multilingual topic model (MLTM); (2) document embeddings derived from cross-lingual reduced rank ridge regression or Cr5 (Josifoski et al., 2019) and; (3) Wasserstein distance for CLDR (Balikas et al., 2018). These methods link documents across languages in fundamentally different ways. MLTM induces a shared cross-lingual topic space and represents documents as a language-independent distribution over these topics; Cr5 obtains cross-lingual document embeddings; and the Wasserstein distance as used by (Balikas et al., 2018) computes distances between documents as sets of cross-lingual word embeddings (Speer et al., 2016). The methods broadly cover the landscape of recent CLDR methods. To our

knowledge, this is the first comparison of Cr5 and Wasserstein for ad hoc retrieval.

This paper adds to the literature on CLDR in three ways: (1) evaluating unsupervised methods for retrieving related documents across languages (ad hoc retrieval), in contrast to retrieval of a single corresponding document; (2) evaluating different ensembling methods; and (3) demonstrating the effectiveness of relating documents across languages through complementary methods.

2. Related Work

Previous work on linking documents across languages has used translation-based features, where the query is translated into the target language and the retrieval task proceeds in the target language (Hull and Grefenstette, 1996; Litschko et al., 2018; Utiyama and Isahara, 2003). Other methods used term-frequency correlation (Tao and Zhai, 2005; Vu et al., 2009), sentence alignment (Utiyama and Isahara, 2003), and named entities (Montalvo et al., 2006). In this paper, we are interested in language-independent models with minimal reliance on lexical resources and other metadata or annotations.

2.1. Multilingual topic model

The multilingual topic model (MLTM) is an extension of LDA topic modelling (Blei et al., 2003) for comparable multilingual corpora (De Smet and Moens, 2009; Mimno et al., 2009). In contrast to LDA, which learns topics by treating each document as independent, MLTM relies on a topically aligned corpus, which consists of tuples of documents in different languages discussing the same themes. MLTM learns separate but aligned topic distributions over the vocabularies of the languages represented in the corpus. One of the main advantages of MLTM is that it can extend across any number of languages, not just two, as long as there is a topically aligned corpus covering these languages. This can be difficult because aligning corpora is not a trivial task, especially as the number of languages gets larger. For this reason, Wikipedia, currently in more than 200 languages, is a popular source of training data for MLTM. Another issue facing topic models is that the choice of hyperparameters can significantly affect the quality and nature of topics extracted from the corpus and, consequently, its performance in the downstream task we want use it for. There are three main hyperparameters in LDA-based models: the number of topics to extract, K; the document concentration parameter, α, that controls the sparsity of the topics associated with each document; and the topic concentration parameter, β, which controls the sparsity of the topic-specific distribution over the vocabulary.

2.2. Cross-lingual document embeddings

Cross-lingual reduced-rank ridge regression (Cr5) was recently introduced as a novel method of obtaining cross-lingual document embeddings (Josifoski et al., 2019). The authors formulate the problem of inducing a shared document embedding space as a linear classification problem. Documents in a multilingual corpus are assigned language-independent concepts. The linear classifier is trained to assign the concepts to documents, learning a matrix of weights W that embeds documents in a concept space close to other documents labelled with the same concept and far from documents expressing different concepts.

They train on a multilingual Wikipedia corpus, where articles are assigned labels based on language-independent Wikipedia concepts. They show that the method outperforms the state-of-the-art cross-lingual document embedding method from previous literature (Litschko et al., 2018). Cr5 is trained to produce document embeddings, but can also be used to obtain embeddings for smaller units, such as sentences and words. One disadvantage is that it requires labelled documents for training. However, the induced cross-lingual vectors can then be used for any tasks in which the input document is made up of words in the vocabulary of the corresponding language in the training set.

2.3. Wasserstein distances for documents

Wasserstein distance is a distance metric between probability distributions and has been previously used to compute distances between text documents in the same language (*Word Mover's Distance* (Kusner et al., 2015)). In (Balikas et al., 2018) the authors propose the Wasserstein distance to compute distances between documents from different languages. Each document is a set of cross-lingual word embeddings (Speer et al., 2016) and each word is associated with some weight, such as its term frequency inverse document frequency (tf.idf). The Wasserstein distance is then the minimum cost of transforming all the words in a query document to the words in a target document. They then demonstrate that using a regularized version of the Wasserstein distance makes the optimization problem faster to solve and, more importantly, allows multiple associations between words in the query and target documents.

3. Experimental setup

3.1. Task and dataset

We evaluate using a dataset of Finnish and Swedish news articles published by the Finnish broadcaster YLE and freely available for download from the Finnish Language Bank[1]. The articles are from 2012-18 and are written separately in the two languages (not translations and not parallel). This dataset contains 604,297 articles in Finnish and

	MLTM Train set	Test set	
	articles per lang	**#candidates**	**#related**
2012	7.2K	-	-
2013	7.2K	1.3K	19.5
2014	7.2K	1.4K	31.8
2015	-	1.5K	35.9

Table 1: Statistics of the training set for training MLTMs and test sets for each year. #candidates is the average size of the candidate articles set and #related is the average number of Swedish articles related to each Finnish article.

228,473 articles in Swedish. Each article is tagged with a set of keywords describing the subject of the article. These keywords were assigned to the articles by a combination of automated methods and manual curation. The keywords vary in specificity, from named entities, such as *Sauli Niinisto* (the Finnish president), to general subjects, such as *talous* (sv: *ekonomi*, en: economy). On average, Swedish articles are tagged with five keywords and 15 keywords for Finnish articles. Keywords are provided in Finnish and Swedish regardless of the article language so no additional mapping is required.

To build a corpus of related news articles for testing, we associate one Finnish article with one or more Swedish articles if they share three or more keywords and if the articles are published in the same month. From this we create three separate test sets: 2013, 2014, and 2015. For each month, we take 100 Finnish articles to use as queries, providing all of the related Swedish articles as a candidate set visible to the models.

To build a topically aligned corpus for training MLTM, we match a Finnish article with a Swedish article if they were published within two days of each other and share three or more keywords. As a result no Finnish article is matched with more than one Swedish article and vice-versa so that we have a set of aligned unique article pairs. To train MLTM we use a year which is preceding the testing year: e.g., we train a model using articles from 2012 and test it on articles from 2013. Unaligned articles are not used for either training or testing. The script for article alignment will be provided in the Github repository for this work.

Table 1 shows the statistics of the training and test sets. As can be seen in the last column of the table, one Finnish article corresonds to almost twenty Swedish articles for the 2013 dataset and more than thirty for the other two datasets. This is typical for large news collections, since one article may have an arbitrary number of related articles. Thus, our corpus is more suitable for ad-hoc search evaluation than Wikipedia or Europarl corpus, since they contain only one-to-one relation[2].

3.2. Models

We use our in-house implementation of MLTM training using Gibbs sampling[3]. The training corpus was tokenized, lemmatized and stopwords were removed. We limited the

---

[1]https://www.kielipankki.fi/corpora/

[2]CLEF 2000-2003 ad-hoc retrieval Test Suite, which also contains many-to-many relations, is not freely available
[3]https://github.com/ezosa/cross-lingual-linking.git

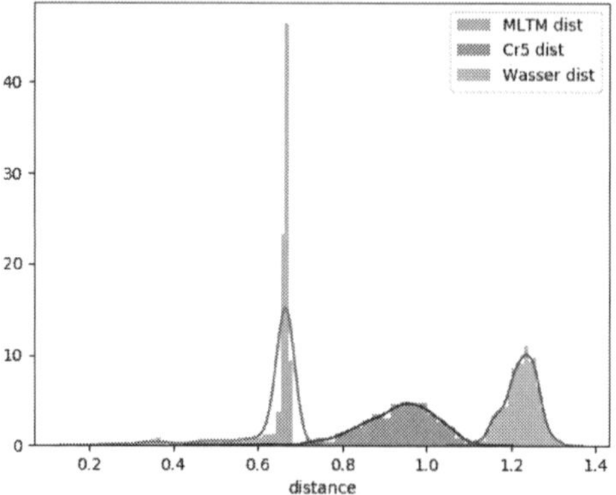

Figure 1: Density plots of the distances between one query document and the candidate documents.

vocabulary to the 9,000 most frequent terms for each language. We train three separate models for 2012, 2013, and 2014 (for the 2013, 2014, and 2015 test sets, respectively). We train all three models with $K = 100$ topics, $\alpha = 1/K$ and $\beta = 0.08$. We use 1,000 iterations for burn-in and then infer vectors for unseen documents by sampling every 25th iteration for 200 iterations. To obtain distances between documents, we compute the Jensen-Shannon (JS) divergence between the document-topic distributions of the query document and each of the candidate documents.

For Cr5, we use pretrained word embeddings for Finnish and Swedish provided by the authors[4]. We construct document embeddings according to the original method – by summing up the embeddings of the words in the document weighted by their frequency. We compute the distance between documents as the cosine distance of the document embeddings.

For Wasserstein distance, we use code provided by the authors for computing distances between documents and use the same cross-lingual embeddings they did in their experiments[5] (Speer et al., 2016). Wasserstein distance has a regularization parameter λ that controls how the model matches words in the query and candidate documents. The authors suggested using $\lambda = 0.1$ because it encourages more relaxed associations between words. Higher values of λ create stronger associations while too low values fail to associate words that are direct translations of each other. In this task, it might make more sense to use lower λ values, though an experiment with $\lambda = 0.01$ brought no noticeable improvement in performance (see Section 3.3.).

We created ensemble models by averaging the document distances from the stand-alone models and ranking candidate documents according to this score. We construct four ensemble models by combining each pair of models, as well as all three: **MLTM_Wass**; **Cr5_Wass**; **MLTM_Cr5**; and **MLTM_Cr5_Wass**.

3.3. Results and Discussion

Table 2 shows the results for each model and ensemble on each of the three test sets, reporting the precision of the top-ranked k results and mean reciprocal rank (MRR). Cr5 is the best-performing stand-alone model by a large margin. Cr5 was originally designed for creating cross-lingual document embeddings by classifying Wikipedia documents according to concepts. We did not retrain it for our particular task. Nevertheless, using these pre-trained word embeddings we were able to retrieve articles that discuss similar subjects in this different domain. However, it is worth noting that Cr5 can only be trained on languages for which labels are available for *some* similarly transferable training domain.

MLTM, being a topic-based model, would seem like the obvious choice for a task like this because we want to find articles that share some broad characteristics with the query document, even if they do not discuss the same named entities or use similar words. However, Cr5 outperforms MLTM on its own. One reason may be that 100 topics are too few. We chose this number because it seemed to give topics that are specific enough for short articles but still broad enough that they could reasonably be used to describe similar articles. Another drawback of this model is that it does not handle out-of-vocabulary words and the choice of using a vocabulary of 9,000 terms might be too low.

Wasserstein distance is the worst-performing of the stand-alone models especially for the 2014 and 2015 test sets where it offers little improvement when ensembled with Cr5 (Cr5_Wass). A possible reason is that it attempts to transform one document to another and therefore favors documents that share a similar vocabulary to the query document. The technique might be suitable for matching Wikipedia articles, as shown in (Balikas et al., 2018) because they talk about the same subject at a fine-grained level and use similar words, whilst in our task the goal is to make broader connections between documents.

In Figure 1, the density plots of the distances of one query document and the candidate documents. We see that MLTM and Wasserstein tend to have sharper peaks while Cr5 distances are flatter. MLTM has minimum and maximum distances of 0.2 and 0.68, respectively, while Cr5 has 0.49 and 1.14, and Wasserstein has 1.08 and 1.34. Topic modelling tends to predict that most of the target documents are far from the query document (peaks at the right side). This is not only true for this particular query document but for other query documents in our test set as well. We also see that Wasserstein has larger distances which is potentially problematic. We tried normalizing the distances produced by the models such that they are centered at zero and using these distances for the ensembled model however it produces the same document rankings as the unnormalized distances. This might be because we are only concerned with the documents with the smallest distances where Wasserstein does not contribute much.

For the ensemble models, combining all three models per-

---

[4]https://github.com/epfl-dlab/Cr5
[5]https://github.com/balikasg/WassersteinRetrieval

Test set:	2013				2014				2015			
Measure:	**P@1**	**P@5**	**P@10**	**MRR**	**P@1**	**P@5**	**P@10**	**MRR**	**P@1**	**P@5**	**P@10**	**MRR**
MLTM	21.8	18.2	16.3	31.6	24.1	22.4	20.6	34.8	30.8	29.0	27.1	41.6
Wass	21.1	13.7	11.3	30.8	21.0	16.9	14.7	31.9	25.1	20.6	17.9	37.2
Wass $\lambda = 0.01$	20.3	13.5	11.1	30.0	21.3	16.8	14.6	32.0	25.1	20.1	17.3	36.6
Cr5	32.5	24.5	21.2	41.7	38.3	30.2	26.0	48.0	43.1	37.1	33.5	53.8
MLTM_Wass	24.6	21.3	19.1	35.2	27.3	25.5	23.4	38.2	30.4	31.4	30.1	42.9
Cr5_Wass	35.4	27.4	23.2	45.2	38.1	32.2	28.2	49.2	41.2	37.7	34.9	52.9
MLTM_Cr5	36.4	28.2	24.4	46.6	**44.8**	34.3	30.1	53.6	42.7	40.1	36.9	54.5
MLTM_Cr5_Wass	**40.7**	**30.7**	**26.3**	**50.3**	43.0	**36.1**	**31.9**	**53.8**	**44.5**	**41.3**	**38.5**	**55.9**

Table 2: Precision at k and MRR of cross-lingual linking of related news articles obtained by three stand-alone models and four ensemble models.

Test set:	2013	2014	2015	AVG
MLTM, Wass	-0.039	-0.016	-0.022	-0.026
Cr5, Wass	0.128	0.027	0.026	0.060
MLTM, Cr5	0.156	0.164	0.178	0.166

Table 3: Mean Spearman correlation of the ranks of candidate documents for each pair of models.

forms best overall for all three test sets and all but one precision level—the only exception is P1 for 2014 where MLTM_Cr5 achieves roughly the same performance. This tells us that each model sometimes finds relevant documents not found by the other models. The correlation of candidate document rankings between the different methods is quite low (Table 3). We compute the correlation between the ranks for each of the 1200 query documents (100 queries for each month) for each year of our test set and average them. As can be seen in the table the correlations are rather low, which means that they retrieve documents based on different principles. The highest correlation is between **MLTM** has the **Cr5** while correlation between **MLTM** and **Wass** is the lowest.

This suggests that there are different ways of retrieving related documents across languages and that the three methods of cross-lingual embeddings, cross-lingual topic spaces and cross-lingual distance measures capture complementary notions of similarity. A simple combination of their decisions is thus able to make better judgements than any can make on its own.

As an example, in Table 4 we show excerpts from a query article in Finnish and some of the related Swedish articles correctly predicted by the different models. For this article, Cr5 gave 10 correct predictions in its top 10 (perfect precision), MLTM gave 8 correct predictions and Wasserstein only 4. Like Cr5, the ensemble model MLTM_Cr5_Wass also achieved perfect precision. MLTM and MLTM_Cr5_Wass shared 4 correct predictions while Cr5 and MLTM_Cr5_Wass shared 7. All the articles correctly predicted by Wasserstein were also predicted by the other models. We show articles from Cr5, MLTM and MLTM_Cr5_Wass that was correctly predicted by that model only and for Wasserstein, we show the top correct article that it predicted.

4. Conclusions and Future work

In this paper we compare three different methods for cross-lingual ad hoc document retrieval by applying them to the task of retrieving Swedish news articles that are related to a given Finnish article. We show that a word-embedding based model, Cr5, performs best followed by the multilingual topic model and the distance-based Wasserstein model has the worst results of the stand-alone models. We then demonstrate that combining at least two of these methods by averaging their distances yields better results than the models used on their own. Finally we show that combining the three models yields the best results. These results tell us that relating documents based on different techniques such as embedding-based or topic-based techniques yields different results and that pooling these results make for a better model.

In the future we plan to investigate the performance of word embedding-based multilingual topic models in this task. There is already some work done on developing topic models that use word embeddings (Batmanghelich et al., 2016; Das et al., 2015). To our knowledge, they have not yet been applied to cross-lingual embeddings. Such a model could potentially combine the benefits of the multilingual topic model with word embeddings for retrieving similar documents across languages.

We also plan to further experiments with multilingual topic models for languages where the amount of linked documents is scarce. In this work, we trained the topic model with thousands of linked articles because the articles were annotated with tags however this might not always be the case, for instance with historical data sets or under-resourced languages where there are not readily available annotated data and manual annotation is time-consuming or requires expert knowledge. In such cases, we could still train a multilingual topic model with smaller amounts of aligned training data or perhaps a training set where some articles do not have a counterpart article in the other language.

There is also scope for further exploration of ensemble methods, going beyond the simple combination of distance metrics we have applied here. As well as combining models in different ways, further, potentially complementary,

Query article	Yleisradion YleX-kanavan kymmenen suosituimman kappaleen listalla,valtaosa on suomalaisartisteja tai -yhtyeitä. Radio Suomen kaikki,kymmenen eniten kuultua kappaletta ovat odotetusti kotimaisia. YleX ja Radio Suomi ovat koonneet listan eniten soittamastaan musiikista vuonna 2012.
MLTM	På min låtlista finns låtar som på olika sätt och från olika perspektiv beskriver livets grundläggande vemod eller "life bitter-sweet", som man brukar säga på Irland. Det säger Tom Sjöblom, som har valt musiken denna vecka i [Min musik.]
Cr5	De isländska banden tar över världen, vi träffade Sóley som nyligen varit på USA-turné med sina isländska kollegor Of Monsters And Men. **Sóley** är isländska och betyder solros. Sóley är också namnet på sångerskan som är en av de mest intressanta nya musikexporterna som kommit från Island.
Wasserstein	Både Radio Vega och Radio Extrem har börjat spela låtar som tävlar i Tävlingen för ny musik UMK. Radio Extrem har tagit in både Krista Siegfrids _Marry me__ och Diandras _Colliding into you__ på spellistan, och låtarna kommer att spelas två gånger om dagen åtminstone nu i början.
MLTM_Cr5_Wass	Smakproven på 30 sekunder av de tolv UMK låtarna kittlade fantasin så,där passligt, men nu behöver vi inte längre gissa oss till hur sångerna,låter i sin helhet. De färdigt producerade bidragen kan nu höras på,Arenan.

Table 4: Excerpt from a query Finnish article and some related Swedish articles correctly predicted by the models. The query article is about popular songs on Finnish radio.

measures of document similarity could be included: for example, explicitly taking into account overlap of named entities, or document publishing metadata if such information is available.

Acknowledgements

This work has been supported by the European Union's Horizon 2020 research and innovation programme under grant 770299 (NewsEye) and 825153 (EMBEDDIA).

References

Balikas, G., Laclau, C., Redko, I., and Amini, M.-R. (2018). Cross-lingual document retrieval using regularized Wasserstein distance. In *European Conference on Information Retrieval*, pages 398–410. Springer.

Batmanghelich, K., Saeedi, A., Narasimhan, K., and Gershman, S. (2016). Nonparametric spherical topic modeling with word embeddings. In *Proceedings of the conference. Association for Computational Linguistics. Meeting*, volume 2016, page 537. NIH Public Access.

Blei, D. M., Ng, A. Y., and Jordan, M. I. (2003). Latent Dirichlet Allocation. *Journal of machine Learning research*, 3(Jan):993–1022.

Das, R., Zaheer, M., and Dyer, C. (2015). Gaussian LDA for topic models with word embeddings. In *Proceedings of the 53rd Annual Meeting of the Association for Computational Linguistics and the 7th International Joint Conference on Natural Language Processing (Volume 1: Long Papers)*, pages 795–804.

De Smet, W. and Moens, M.-F. (2009). Cross-language linking of news stories on the web using interlingual topic modelling. In *Proceedings of the 2nd ACM workshop on Social web search and mining*, pages 57–64. ACM.

Hull, D. A. and Grefenstette, G. (1996). Querying across languages: a dictionary-based approach to multilingual information retrieval. In *Proceedings of the 19th annual international ACM SIGIR conference on Research and development in information retrieval*, pages 49–57. Citeseer.

Josifoski, M., Paskov, I. S., Paskov, H. S., Jaggi, M., and West, R. (2019). Crosslingual document embedding as reduced-rank ridge regression. In *Proceedings of the Twelfth ACM International Conference on Web Search and Data Mining*, pages 744–752. ACM.

Kusner, M., Sun, Y., Kolkin, N., and Weinberger, K. (2015). From word embeddings to document distances. In *International conference on machine learning*, pages 957–966.

Litschko, R., Glavaš, G., Ponzetto, S. P., and Vulić, I. (2018). Unsupervised cross-lingual information retrieval using monolingual data only. In *The 41st International ACM SIGIR Conference on Research & Development in Information Retrieval*, pages 1253–1256. ACM.

Litschko, R., Glavaš, G., Vulic, I., and Dietz, L. (2019). Evaluating resource-lean cross-lingual embedding models in unsupervised retrieval. In *Proceedings of the 42nd International ACM SIGIR Conference on Research and Development in Information Retrieval*, pages 1109–1112. ACM.

Mimno, D., Wallach, H. M., Naradowsky, J., Smith, D. A., and McCallum, A. (2009). Polylingual topic models. In *Proceedings of the 2009 Conference on Empirical Methods in Natural Language Processing: Volume 2-Volume 2*, pages 880–889. Association for Computational Linguistics.

Montalvo, S., Martinez, R., Casillas, A., and Fresno, V. (2006). Multilingual document clustering: an heuristic approach based on cognate named entities. In *Proceedings of the 21st International Conference on Computational Linguistics and the 44th annual meeting of the Association for Computational Linguistics*, pages 1145–1152. Association for Computational Linguistics.

Speer, R., Chin, J., and Havasi, C. (2016). ConceptNet 5.5: An open multilingual graph of general knowledge. *CoRR*, abs/1612.03975.

Tao, T. and Zhai, C. (2005). Mining comparable bilingual text corpora for cross-language information integration. In *Proceedings of the eleventh ACM SIGKDD interna-

tional conference on Knowledge discovery in data mining, pages 691–696. ACM.

Utiyama, M. and Isahara, H. (2003). Reliable measures for aligning Japanese-English news articles and sentences. In *Proceedings of the 41st Annual Meeting on Association for Computational Linguistics-Volume 1*, pages 72–79. Association for Computational Linguistics.

Voorhees, E. (2003). Overview of TREC 2003. pages 1–13, 01.

Vu, T., Aw, A. T., and Zhang, M. (2009). Feature-based method for document alignment in comparable news corpora. In *Proceedings of the 12th Conference of the European Chapter of the Association for Computational Linguistics*, pages 843–851. Association for Computational Linguistics.

Wang, Y.-C., Wu, C.-K., and Tsai, R. T.-H. (2016). Cross-language article linking with different knowledge bases using bilingual topic model and translation features. *Knowledge-Based Systems*, 111:228–236.

Proceedings of the Cross-Language Search and Summarization of Text and Speech Workshop, pages 38–43
Language Resources and Evaluation Conference (LREC 2020), Marseille, 11–16 May 2020
© European Language Resources Association (ELRA), licensed under CC-BY-NC

Reformulating Information Retrieval from Speech and Text as a Detection Problem

Damianos Karakos[†], Rabih Zbib[*], William Hartmann[†], Richard Schwartz[†], John Makhoul[†]
[†]Raytheon BBN Technologies, Cambridge, MA
[*]Avature, Spain
[†]e-mail: {damianos.karakos, william.hartmann, rich.schwartz, john.makhoul}@raytheon.com
[*]rabih.zbib@avature.net

Abstract

In the IARPA MATERIAL program, information retrieval (IR) is treated as a hard detection problem; the system has to output a single global ranking over *all* queries, and apply a hard threshold on this global list to come up with all the hypothesized relevant documents. This means that how queries are ranked *relative to each other* can have a dramatic impact on performance. In this paper, we study such a performance measure, the Average Query Weighted Value (AQWV), which is a combination of miss and false alarm rates. AQWV requires that the same detection threshold is applied to all queries. Hence, detection scores of different queries should be *comparable*, and, to do that, a *score normalization* technique (commonly used in keyword spotting from speech) should be used. We describe unsupervised methods for score normalization, which are borrowed from the speech field and adapted accordingly for IR, and demonstrate that they greatly improve AQWV on the task of cross-language information retrieval (CLIR), on three low-resource languages used in MATERIAL. We also present a novel supervised score normalization approach which gives additional gains.

1. Introduction

When an information retrieval system is used as a support tool in a decision-making process, the user is mainly interested in whether the data under consideration contains (or, is relevant to) any of the queries of interest. For example, consider the case of streaming audio where actions must be made based upon a query detection. As each document is processed, a binary decision must be made about relevance for each query[1]. Clearly, when dealing with a decision operation, the most appropriate way to measure system performance (from an operational viewpoint) is to incorporate the two error sources that affect a user's experience: misses and false alarms. Minimizing a linear combination of these two errors is a very reasonable optimization objective, and it was chosen by the IARPA MATERIAL program as the main performance measure. Specifically, the AQWV measure is defined as follows:

$$AQWV = 1 - \overline{\text{pMiss}} - \beta \, \overline{\text{pFA}}. \qquad (1)$$

$\overline{\text{pMiss}}$ is the average per-query miss rate and is defined as follows

$$\overline{\text{pMiss}} = \frac{1}{|Q_r|} \sum_{q \in Q_r} \frac{\text{\# misses of } q}{\text{\# refs of } q}, \qquad (2)$$

where Q_r is the set of queries with references in the data (i.e., each has at least one relevant document). The number of references and the number of misses of query q is computed based on the whole document collection $\mathscr{C}$ under consideration.

$\overline{\text{pFA}}$, the average per-query false alarm rate, is defined as follows

$$\overline{\text{pFA}} = \frac{1}{|Q|} \sum_{q \in Q} \frac{\text{\# FAs of } q}{|\mathscr{C}| - \text{\# refs of } q}, \qquad (3)$$

The constant β in Equation (1) changes the relative importance of the two types of error ($\beta = 40$ in MATERIAL). Note that this measure assumes a single decision threshold, which means that all detection scores, over all queries, have to be commensurate. In this paper, we present techniques for transforming the detection scores that are generated by an IR system so that they are comparable across queries. The paper is organized as follows: Section 2 gives a short summary of previous work on score normalization. Section 3 presents a supervised method for score normalization, adapted to IR. Section 4 describes the experimental setup and presents results on three low-resource languages used in the IARPA MATERIAL program: Somali, Swahili and Tagalog. Finally, Section 5 contains concluding remarks.

2. Related Work

AQWV is very similar to the Average Term Weighted Value (ATWV) (Fiscus et al., 2007), which was first used in the NIST 2006 Spoken Term Detection evaluation and then in the IARPA BABEL program (Bab, 2011) for keyword spotting from speech. As was argued in (Karakos et al., 2013) and elsewhere, generating commensurate detection scores is important for optimizing this performance measure. The main difference between ATWV and AQWV is in the granularity of the detections: keyword spotting tries to find all occurrences of a keyword of interest, no matter how many times it is spoken in a speech document. By contrast, the IR task we consider here is about retrieving whole documents that contain the query of interest, but without the need to pinpoint its exact location in the document. In other words, the granularity of the keyword spotting task is at the second (or fraction of second) level, while the granularity of the information retrieval task is at the document level. So, when computing the denominators in pMiss and pFA, AQWV uses number of documents, not number of occurrences or number of seconds as in ATWV. For this reason, the range of AQWV is $[-\beta, 1]$ (as opposed to $(-\infty, 1]$ for ATWV). (Wegmann et al., 2013) contains a detailed discussion of ATWV; most of the salient points also apply to

---

[*]While at Raytheon BBN Technologies.

[1]We are using document-level granularity in this paper, although similar techniques can be used for different granularities as well.

AQWV.

A number of *unsupervised* score normalization approaches have been developed for keyword spotting. pFA normalization was introduced in (Zhang et al., 2012) and used again in (Karakos et al., 2013). Keyword-specific thresholds (KST) (Karakos et al., 2013) is the most principled approach, as it is derived from fundamental theorems of decision theory. Sum-to-one (STO) (Wu, 2012; Mamou et al., 2013) is yet another popular approach, which was initially applied to problems in IR and later to keyword spotting. An in-depth comparison of these last two techniques appears in (Wang and Metze, 2014), and, since we use them in our experiments, we give more details about them below (KST is renamed QST for obvious reasons). A version of QST was also used more recently in (Shing et al., 2019) for CLIR as well.

Query-Specific Thresholds (QST)

This method estimates a query-specific threshold $t(q)$, assuming the un-normalized scores are *posterior probabilities* or posterior-like numbers between 0 and 1. As mentioned in Section 1, the AQWV and ATWV metrics are similar, allowing us to use the same optimality reasoning to compute query-specific thresholds $t(q)$. Decision theory tells us that the optimal threshold is where the expected cost of a false alarm and miss are equal. With some algebra, it can be shown that the "optimal" decision thresholds are given by:

$$t^*(q) = \frac{\beta \, N_{\text{true}}(q)}{|\mathscr{C}| + (\beta - 1) N_{\text{true}}(q)} \tag{4}$$

where $N_{\text{true}}(q)$ is the number of documents that are truly relevant to query q. This number is unknown, but it can be approximated by the sum of posteriors over the whole collection, i.e.,

$$N_{\text{sum}}(q) = \sum_{d \in \mathscr{C}} score(q, d), \tag{5}$$

where $score(q, d)$ is the retrieval score returned by the core IR system for query q and document d. Then, the normalized scores can either be given by a linear shift, or by the non-linear transformation mentioned in (Karakos et al., 2013)

$$score_{\text{qst}} = \exp\left\{ -\frac{\log(score)}{\log(t^*(q))} \right\}, \tag{6}$$

which makes the common decision threshold for all queries equal to $1/e \approx 0.3679$. This is the decision threshold we use for computing AQWV in the QST results of Section 4.

Sum-to-One Score (STO)

This method, mentioned in (Wu, 2012; Mamou et al., 2013), performs a per-query normalization so that the normalized detections of a query *over the whole document collection* sum to one. In other words,

$$score_{\text{sto}} = \frac{score}{N_{\text{sum}}(q)}, \tag{7}$$

where $N_{\text{sum}}(q)$ is given by (5). Unlike QST, this method does not produce a decision threshold. As mentioned

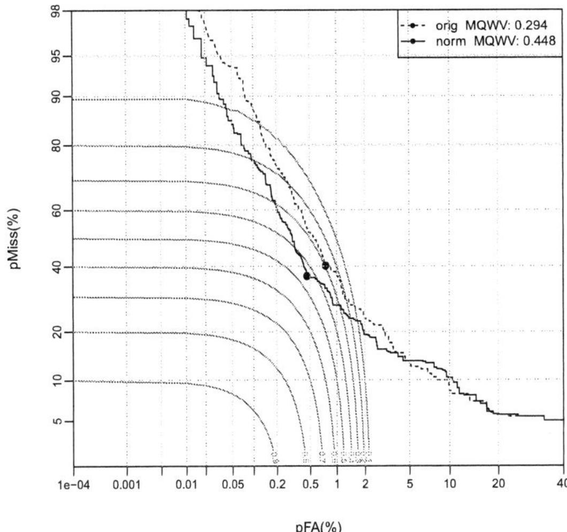

Figure 1: Comparison of the DET curves without/with score normalization. The gray lines are contours of equal AQWV.

in (Mamou et al., 2013), the decision threshold can be determined based on performance on a tuning set. In our experiments, we estimate the decision threshold on the training set and apply it on the two other datasets (Tune/Test).

Previous Supervised Techniques

Supervised (machine learning) techniques for score normalization focused on extracting a number of features and using them in a discriminative learning framework to directly compute the probability that a keyword is present in a specific location in the audio. For example, the authors in (Wang et al., 2009) used lattice-derived confidence scores as features in a MLP and SVM to come up with calibrated scores that significantly improved ATWV. In (Pham et al., 2014), they used features such as posterior probability, number of vowels, how many other competing arcs were present in the ASR lattice, etc., in a MLP to compute posterior-like scores, which were subsequently normalized with KST or STO. In (Lv et al., 2016), the features used were just the original posterior and KST-normalized score, but these were computed a few times, using different subword units. Finally, in (Soto et al., 2014), a large number of features (both related to posteriors in confusion networks and their transformations, as well features derived from acoustics, phonetic dictionary, etc.) was used in a SVM framework, which led to significant improvements over the unsupervised methods.

Many references related to keyword spotting and score normalization can also be found in (Tejedor et al., 2015).

Figure 1 shows a comparison of the DET curves for the un-normalized and normalized outputs of a CLIR system. There is a significant gain from normalization, especially around the range of values where the maximum AQWV (i.e., MQWV) is attained.

3. Supervised Score Normalization

Our approach to supervised score normalization is to (i) use an optimization framework that directly optimizes the measure of interest (AQWV), and (ii) use features that are both functions of the query and the document, without making any assumptions about whether we deal with speech or text (our approach has to be able to work well with both, so, it cannot rely on the presence of speech lattices or confusion networks, in contrast to the aforementioned approaches). We generate several features—functions of the corpus, query, and the original retrieval score—and then weight them appropriately. We learn the feature weights so that, when thresholded, the combined score maximizes the performance metric.

We assume that each query-document pair (q, d) in the training data is labeled for relevance (0/1). We compute a number of features, such as the log of the following quantities:

- Original retrieval $score(q, d)$

- The QST-transformed score $score_{qst}(q, d)$

- The normalized sum $N_{sum}(q)/|\mathcal{C}|$

- The three features:

$$\min_{w \in q}\{score(w, d)\},\ \max_{w \in q}\{score(w, d)\},\ \operatorname*{avg}_{w \in q}\{score(w, d)\},$$

  where avg_w is just the average over all words w in query q (esp. for multi-word queries).

- The three features:

$$\min_{w \in q}\{count(w)\},\ \max_{w \in q}\{count(w)\},\ \operatorname*{avg}_{w \in q}\{count(w)\},$$

  where $count(w)$ is the count of w in the IR training data (e.g., parallel data used to train the bilingual dictionary for CLIR).

The above features $f_1, \ldots, f_F$, together with the binary labels, are fed into an optimizer that uses Powell's method (Press et al., 2007), with the goal to learn feature weights $\boldsymbol{\alpha} = (\alpha_1, \ldots, \alpha_F)$, as well as an optimal decision threshold t^* that maximize AQWV. At each optimization iteration, the weights are used to compute new retrieval scores

$$score_{model}(q, d) = \sum_{i=1}^{F} \alpha_i \cdot f_i$$

and new decisions

$$decision(q, d) = \mathbf{1}[score_{model}(q, d) \geq t^*].$$

During training, AQWV performance is also measured on a "tuning" set for early stopping. L2 regularization (which forces the trained weights to have small absolute values, to reduce the risk of overfitting) can also be used by changing the optimization criterion to

$$AQWV(\boldsymbol{\alpha}, t) - \lambda \cdot L2(\boldsymbol{\alpha}).$$

	Text			Audio		
	Train	Tune	Test	Train	Tune	Test
Somali	338	482	478	142	213	222
Swahili	316	449	493	155	217	207
Tagalog	291	460	-	171	244	-

Table 1: Size of various datasets (in terms of number of documents).

Note that some of the above features are dependent on various basic properties of the corpus (e.g., number of documents) and of the query set (e.g., OOV rate). In this paper, we do not study the effect of mismatched train/test conditions that may arise, for instance, when train and test corpora are significantly different. A test set that is an order of magnitude larger than the training set can cause significant mismatch in the train/test feature distributions, for the corpus-dependent features we described earlier (such as the QST-transformed score and the normalized sum). We plan to investigate such scenarios in future work.

Finally, note that, in lieu of Powell's method, we have also used a MLP framework. However, given that the data on which we train the learner is small, we did not manage to obtain results that generalized better.

4. Experimental Results

4.1. Query Sets and Retrieval Corpora

To show the benefit of normalization and thresholding to IR, we report experimental results on a Cross-language IR (CLIR) task from three different languages to English: Somali, Swahili and Tagalog. Using data from the IARPA MATERIAL program, we report on retrieval of Text and Speech documents. For each genre, we consider three data and query set conditions: (i) **Train:** A training data set D_{Train} and a training query set Q_{Train} are used for training the normalization model of Section 3 as well as decision thresholds. (ii) **Tune:** A tuning set D_{Tune} is used, together with Q_{Train}, for evaluating the stopping criterion. (iii) **Test:** Unseen data set D_{Test} and unseen query set Q_{Test} are used to assess blind performance. Statistics of these corpora appear in Table 1. As for the query set sizes, all languages have the same number of queries: Q_{Train} consists of 300 queries and Q_{Test} consists of 1000 queries.

4.2. The CLIR System

We give a brief description of the CLIR system that is used to generate the original retrieval scores. A more detailed description appears in (Zbib et al., 2019). It uses a probabilistic bilingual dictionary, trained on a set of parallel sentences and lexicons that were aligned with GIZA++ (Och and Ney, 2003). For each language pair (Somali-English, Swahili-English and Tagalog-English) the bilingual dictionary provides a translation probability $P(e|f)$ between a source word f and a target word e. Queries consist of one or more words in the target language (English), and a document is deemed relevant to a query if it contains at least one occurrence of each of the terms of the query.[2]

---

[2]For this program, each query consists of one or two English terms, each a word or short phrase. In some cases, there are fea-

In mathematical terms, for query q and document d, and assuming that $\mathscr{T}(d)$ is the set of all translations of all words and phrases in d, the CLIR system computes $score(q, d)$ as follows:

$$
\begin{aligned}
&P(d \text{ is relevant to } q) \\
&= P(\text{each term } w \text{ of } q \text{ occurs at least once in } \mathscr{T}(d)) \\
&= \prod_{w \in q} P(w \text{ occurs at least once in } \mathscr{T}(d)) \\
&= \prod_{w \in q} \big(1 - P(w \text{ does not occur in } \mathscr{T}(d))\big) \\
&= \prod_{w \in q} \Big(1 - \prod_{f \in d}(1 - P(w|f))\Big) \quad (8)
\end{aligned}
$$

Note that (Zbib et al., 2019) performs lexical translation of source-language documents to English instead of translation of the (short) English queries to the source language; the longer context in the source documents gives a more accurate translation.

For speech documents, instead of using the translations of the 1-best output of the automatic speech recognition (ASR) system (which could be erroneous) we consider multiple ASR alternatives in the form of a *confusion network*. The latter allows us to have a probabilistic representation of the content of the foreign document, i.e., probability of occurrence $p(f|d)$ for source word f. This can be used seamlessly in (8), giving rise to a modified formula

$$
P(d \text{ is relevant to } q) = \prod_{w \in q} \Big(1 - \prod_{f \in d}(1 - P(f|d) \cdot P(w|f))\Big) \quad (9)
$$

Note that the occurrence probabilities of all English terms in the bilingual dictionary can be pre-computed, and accessed at retrieval time using an efficient indexing scheme.

4.3. Parallel Training Data

Parallel training data were used to estimate the probabilistic dictionaries. The data consist mostly of parallel sentences released under the IARPA MATERIAL and IARPA LORELEI (LOR, 2015) programs. A parallel lexicon downloaded automatically from Panlex (https://panlex.org/) was also included. Training data are completely disjoint from the data mentioned in Section 4.1.

4.4. ASR System Description

The amount of transcribed speech available for acoustic model training varied for each language: 48 hours for Somali, 68 hours for Swahili and 128 hours for Tagalog. For language modeling, automatically collected web data (using the techniques of (Zhang et al., 2015)) were also used. In addition to the MATERIAL data, Swahili and Tagalog also include training data from the IARPA Babel program (Bab, 2011).

---

tures associated with the term that constrain the sense or morphology. A document is relevant if at least one place in the foreign source could be translated to the term(s). In our experiments, the CLIR system simplifies the problem by requiring that each of the terms of the query is a possible translation of at least one foreign word in the document, ignoring any of the semantic or syntactic constraints.

Our ASR systems are trained using the Sage speech processing platform (Hsiao et al., 2016), which integrates multiple machine learning toolkits, and uses Kaldi (Povey et al., 2011) for acoustic model training. Our acoustic models are pre-trained on 1500 hours of data from 11 languages (Keith et al., 2018) and then fine-tuned to the target language. We use a CNN-LSTM acoustic model, which is similar to the TDNN-LSTM (Cheng et al., 2017), but with eight additional convolutional layers prepended to the network.

Language	Baseline	+LM Expansion	+ SST
Somali	60.6	49.4	46.1
Swahili	44.3	33.7	30.1
Tagalog	46.6	33.9	29.6

Table 2: Word error rate (WER) performance on a tuning set (known as Analysis1 in the MATERIAL program). Baseline refers to our multilingual CNN-LSTM acoustic model. LM Expansion expands the LM and lexicon using the automatically collected web data. SST further improves the acoustic model with semi-supervised training.

While word error rate (WER) is not the metric of interest, we show WER results in Table 2 to give a sense of the task difficulty. Our baseline results use our best acoustic model with the given training data, but the WER is still over 40% for each language. A major difficulty for ASR in the IARPA MATERIAL program is the mismatch between the training and test data. All training data is conversational telephone speech (CTS), while the test data is mostly broadcast data. Expanding the language model (LM) with the collected web data partially overcomes this mismatch and gives more than a 10 point absolute improvement in WER. We further reduce the mismatch through semi-supervised training using the evaluation data (approximately 70 hours). Note that this adaptation is unsupervised and is allowed by the MATERIAL program. During decoding we use standard trigram language models. We perform IR on CNets as it significantly improves performance beyond the one-best.

4.5. AQWV/MQWV Results

Table 3(a) contains AQWV results with the various normalization techniques described in the paper (the column "original" is without normalization), for the Train and Test retrieval corpora mentioned in Section 4.1.

Some observations are in order:

1. Compared to the original system scores, almost all normalization methods give gains on the text genre of all datasets. On the Test condition, the average gain (from the supervised normalization) for the text genre is 258%, while the average gain for the audio genre is 96% relative. This shows that, for measures such as AQWV (that rely on hard decisions) score normalization is of crucial importance.

2. In all cases, the supervised, model-based approach, has the best performance on the Test condition among all methods considered. Compared to the best unsupervised method, the supervised approach is 23% bet-

		Train condition				Tune condition				Test condition			
		orig	QST	STO	model	orig	QST	STO	model	orig	QST	STO	model
Somali	text	7.1	16.9	15.7	**22.6**	8.4	19.9	16.2	**22.3**	-2.9	14.0	13.4	**14.6**
	audio	3.9	-1.5	2.2	**9.9**	-2.9	-2.4	-0.9	**4.5**	-0.4	5.2	2.3	**10.3**
Swahili	text	29.4	39.6	34.7	**44.8**	20.9	38.1	30.8	**38.8**	16.5	33.0	33.8	**34.1**
	audio	29.6	21.1	17.0	**33.0**	20.7	19.4	16.1	**31.1**	20.0	17.9	13.8	**28.2**
Tagalog	text	45.7	53.5	48.9	**59.4**	49.8	52.3	47.0	**60.2**	-	-	-	-
	audio	51.1	41.3	39.1	**57.9**	38.8	34.5	31.9	**46.6**	-	-	-	-

(a) AQWV results

		Train condition				Tune condition				Test condition			
		orig	QST	STO	model	orig	QST	STO	model	orig	QST	STO	model
Somali	text	7.1	20.2	15.7	**22.6**	9.3	21.4	16.9	**25.0**	0.2	**16.2**	14.7	15.5
	audio	3.9	8.9	2.2	**9.9**	0.0	3.9	2.9	**4.7**	0.8	**13.1**	**13.1**	11.9
Swahili	text	29.4	40.4	34.7	**44.8**	21.8	38.9	35.0	**39.5**	18.1	33.5	34.1	**35.7**
	audio	29.6	28.3	17.0	**33.0**	21.4	28.6	19.7	**31.8**	21.4	25.6	14.4	**30.0**
Tagalog	text	45.7	54.8	48.9	**59.4**	51.7	55.2	50.6	**60.3**	-	-	-	-
	audio	51.1	55.1	39.1	**57.9**	43.9	43.7	43.2	**48.8**	-	-	-	-

(b) MQWV results

Table 3: (a) AQWV results on two genres of three languages (rows) and three conditions. The best result per dataset is shown in **bold**. (b) Corresponding MQWV results using the oracle decision threshold per condition.

ter (relative) on average over all languages and genres on the Test condition.

3. QST is substantially better than STO in all cases. This is expected, given that QST is designed specifically for AQWV.

Note that, for the Tune and Test conditions, the results of Table 3(a) were obtained with a decision threshold that was optimal on the Train condition. This, of course, can be suboptimal. For example, the AQWV of the original (un-normalized) system for the Somali-text Test condition is negative because the tuned acceptance threshold is too low, which makes the false alarm rate too high (a decision threshold that does not accept anything gives an AQWV of zero). So, to better understand the effect that score normalization has on the performance of a system and remove the error introduced by the imperfect decision threshold, we also computed an oracle AQWV value, the *maximum* AQWV (MQWV), obtained by sweeping over all possible decision thresholds in each one of the conditions presented, which we show in Table 3(b). We see that all MQWV values are now non-negative, and, as expected, greater than the AQWV counterparts of Table 3(a). The supervised method is still the best on average over all languages and conditions (it is worse than QST by 0.95% absolute on Somali Test but better than QST by 3% absolute on Swahili Test).

5. Concluding Remarks

In this paper, we looked at the problem of coming up with producing hard decisions in a CLIR system. One interesting application that we did not have the space to investigate in this paper is where the retrieval is done on-line, in a streaming fashion. Although there is no concept of a "fixed" collection in this case, one can consider a sliding window through the stream for purposes of computing various features, such as the sum of posteriors of Sections 2 and 3. We plan to investigate this problem in a future publication, as well as techniques that integrate score normalization directly into a CLIR engine (e.g., train a neural network CLIR system with the objective to optimize the ultimate measure of interest, instead of an approximate measure such as cross-entropy). Furthermore, with the right architecture, the neural network can come up with the most appropriate features for this task.

6. Acknowledgements

This work was supported by the Intelligence Advanced Research Projects Activity (IARPA) via Department of Defense US Air Force Research Laboratory contract number FA8650-17-C-9118. Useful discussions with other members of the Analytics and Machine Intelligence Department at Raytheon BBN Technologies are gratefully acknowledged.

7. Bibliographical References

(2011). IARPA Babel program - broad agency announcement (baa). https://www.iarpa.gov/index.php/research-programs/babel.

Cheng, G., Peddinti, V., Povey, D., Manohar, V., Khudanpur, S., and Yan, Y. (2017). An exploration of dropout with LSTMs. In *Proc. Interspeech*.

Fiscus, J. G., Ajot, J., and Garofolo, J. S. (2007). Results of the 2006 spoken term detection evaluation.

Hsiao, R., Meermeier, R., Ng, T., Huang, Z., Jordan, M., Kan, E., Alumäe, T., Silovský, J., Hartmann, W., Keith, F., et al. (2016). Sage: The new bbn speech processing platform. In *Interspeech*, pages 3022–3026.

Karakos, D., Schwartz, R., Tsakalidis, S., Zhang, L., Ranjan, S., Ng, T. T., Hsiao, R., Saikumar, G., Bulyko, I., Nguyen, L., et al. (2013). Score normalization and system combination for improved keyword spotting. In *Au-*

tomatic Speech Recognition and Understanding (ASRU), 2013 IEEE Workshop on, pages 210–215. IEEE.

Keith, F., Hartmann, W., Siu, M.-H., Ma, J., and Kimball, O. (2018). Optimizing multilingual knowledge transfer for time-delay neural networks with low-rank factorization. In *2018 IEEE International Conference on Acoustics, Speech and Signal Processing (ICASSP)*, pages 4924–4928. IEEE.

(2015). DARPA LORELEI Program - broad agency announcement (baa). https://www.darpa.mil/program/low-resource-languages-for-emergent-incidents.

Lv, Z., Cai, M., Zhang, W.-Q., and Liu, J. (2016). A novel discriminative score calibration method for keyword search. In *Interspeech*.

Mamou, J., Cui, J., Cui, X., Gales, M. J. F., Kingsbury, B., Knill, K., Mangu, L., Nolden, D., Pickeny, M., Ramabhadran, B., Schlüter, R., Sethy, A., and Woodland, P. C. (2013). Score combination and score normalization for spoken term detection. In *Acoustics, Speech and Signal Processing (ICASSP), 2013 IEEE International Conference on*, pages 8272–8276. IEEE.

Och, F. J. and Ney, H. (2003). A systematic comparison of various statistical alignment models. *Computational Linguistics*, 29(1):19–51.

Pham, V. T., Xu, H., Chen, N. F., Sivadas, S., Lim, B. P., Chng, E. S., and H., L. (2014). Discriminative score normalization for keyword search decision. In *Acoustics, Speech and Signal Processing (ICASSP), 2014 IEEE International Conference on*.

Povey, D., Ghoshal, A., Boulianne, G., Burget, L., Glembek, O., Goel, N., Hannemann, M., Motlicek, P., Qian, Y., Schwarz, P., et al. (2011). The kaldi speech recognition toolkit. In *IEEE 2011 workshop on automatic speech recognition and understanding*, number EPFL-CONF-192584. IEEE Signal Processing Society.

Press, W. H., Teukolsky, S. A., Vetterling, W. T., and Flanery, B. P. (2007). *Numerical Recipes: The Art of Scientific Computing*. Cambridge University Press.

Shing, H.-C., Barrow, J., Galuščáková, P., Oard, D. W., and Resnik, P. (2019). Unsupervised system combination for set-based retrieval with expectation maximization. In Fabio Crestani, et al., editors, *CLEF-2019: Experimental IR Meets Multilinguality, Multimodality, and Interaction*, pages 191–197, Cham. Springer International Publishing.

Soto, V., Mangu, L., Rosenberg, A., and Hirschberg, J. (2014). A comparison of multiple methods for rescoring keyword search lists for low resource languages. In *Interspeech*.

Tejedor, J., Toledano, D. T., Lopez-Otero, P., Docio-Fernandez, L., Garcia-Mateo, C., Cardenal, A., Echeverry-Correa, J. D., Coucheiro-Limeres, A., Olcoz, J., and Miguel, A. (2015). Spoken term detection AL-BAYZIN 2014 evaluation: overview, systems, results, and discussion. *EURASIP Journal on Audio, Speech, and Music Processing*, 2015(1).

Wang, Y. and Metze, F. (2014). An in-depth comparison of keyword specific thresholding and sum-to-one score normalization. In *Interspeech*.

Wang, D., King, S., Frankel, J., and Bell, P. (2009). Term-dependent confidence for out-of-vocabulary term detection. In *Interspeech*.

Wegmann, S., Faria, A., Janin, A., Riedhammer, K., and Morgan, N. (2013). The tao of atwv: Probing the mysteries of keyword search performance. In *2013 IEEE Workshop on Automatic Speech Recognition and Understanding*, pages 192–197. IEEE.

Wu, S. (2012). *Data Fusion in Information Retrieval*. Springer.

Zbib, R., Zhao, L., Karakos, D., Hartmann, W., DeYoung, J., Huang, Z., Jiang, Z., Rivkin, N., Zhang, L., Schwartz, R. M., and Makhoul, J. (2019). Neural-network lexical translation for cross-lingual IR from text and speech. In Benjamin Piwowarski, et al., editors, *Proceedings of the 42nd International ACM SIGIR Conference on Research and Development in Information Retrieval, SIGIR 2019, Paris, France, July 21-25, 2019*, pages 645–654. ACM.

Zhang, B., Schwartz, R., Tsakalidis, S., Nguyen, L., and Matsoukas, S. (2012). White listing and score normalization for keyword spotting of noisy speech. In *Interspeech*.

Zhang, L., Karakos, D., Hartmann, W., Hsiao, R., Schwartz, R., and Tsakalidis, S. (2015). Enhancing low resource keyword spotting with automatically retrieved web documents. In *Interspeech*, pages 839–843.

Proceedings of the Cross-Language Search and Summarization of Text and Speech Workshop, pages 44–51
Language Resources and Evaluation Conference (LREC 2020), Marseille, 11–16 May 2020
© European Language Resources Association (ELRA), licensed under CC-BY-NC

The 2019 BBN Cross-lingual Information Retrieval System

Le Zhang, Damianos Karakos, William Hartmann, Manaj Srivastava
Lee Tarlin, David Akodes, Sanjay Krishna Gouda, Numra Bathool, Lingjun Zhao
Zhuolin Jiang, Richard Schwartz, John Makhoul
Raytheon BBN Technologies
Cambridge MA, USA
{le.zhang,damianos.karakos,william.hartmann,manaj.srivastava}@raytheon.com
{lee.tarlin,david.akodes,sanjaykrishna.gouda,numra.saleem.ahmed.khan,lingjun.zhao}@raytheon.com
{zhuolin.jiang,rich.schwartz,john.makhoul}@raytheon.com

Abstract

In this paper, we describe a cross-lingual information retrieval (CLIR) system that, given a query in English, and a set of audio and text documents in a foreign language, can return a scored list of relevant documents, and present findings in a summary form in English. Foreign audio documents are first transcribed by a state-of-the-art pretrained multilingual speech recognition model that is fine tuned to the target language. For text documents, we use multiple multilingual neural machine translation (MT) models to achieve good translation results, especially for low/medium resource languages. The processed documents and queries are then scored using a probabilistic CLIR model that makes use of the probability of translation from GIZA translation tables and scores from a Neural Network Lexical Translation Model (NNLTM). Additionally, advanced score normalization, combination, and thresholding schemes are employed to maximize the Average Query Weighted Value (AQWV) scores. The CLIR output, together with multiple translation renderings, are selected and translated into English snippets via a summarization model. Our turnkey system is language agnostic and can be quickly trained for a new low-resource language in few days.

Keywords: cross-lingual informational retrieval, average query weighted value, AQWV

1. Introduction

The popularity of the Internet has made it easy to access vast amount of multilingual information for anyone. Yet, it is hard to understand information in a language you do not speak, not to mention searching through it. Cross-Language Information Retrieval (CLIR) and Summarization make it possible to break the language barrier and to make domain information accessible to all users irrespective of language and region.

The IARPA MATERIAL[1] program presents us with the challenge of developing high-performance CLIR, machine translation, automatic speech recognition (ASR), and summarization for a new language in a few weeks, given limited training resources. In this paper, we describe our CLIR system entry to the MATERIAL evaluation of October, 2019. We were to process evaluation data for both Lithuanian and Bulgarian and to submit system output in 10 days.

Our CLIR system achieves the same goal as the SARAL system (Boschee et al., 2019a). While both systems feature a neural network (NN) architecture, the main difference lies in the way an NN model is used. The SARAL system uses a neural network attention model (dot-product) to compute query-document relevance from a shared embedding space, while our system utilizes neural network (multilayer perceptron) as part of the Neural Network Lexical Translation Model (Zbib et al., 2019) to produce probability of translation needed by a probabilistic CLIR model.

The rest of this paper is organized as follows: we introduce the task and data in section 2, including a high level overview of the technical approach. Subsequent sections describe each individual component of the system in more detail. Section 3 and 4 cover Automatic Speech Recogni-

tion and Machine translation, two of the key pre-processing components. The CLIR component is presented in section 5 while Summarization is described in section 6. We present the result in section 7 and discuss the application of the system to low resource languages in section 8. We conclude this paper in section 9.

2. Task and Data

The task of MATERIAL evaluation is given a set of foreign language documents and English queries, retrieve documents that are relevant to each query and generate a summary in English for each document the system deems relevant to the query. Note that the MATERIAL summaries are query-biased, i.e. the purpose of a summary is to allow an English speaker to judge whether the original foreign language document might have been relevant to the query. It is query-biased summary of thoughts not general document summary.

2.1. The AQWV Metric

The main evaluation metric is the Average Query Weighted Value score, a numerical score for every query-document pair, and is defined as a linear combination of the miss and false alarm rates:

$$AQWV = 1 - \left(\overline{\text{pMiss}} + \beta\,\overline{\text{pFA}}\right) \qquad (1)$$

$\overline{\text{pMiss}}$ is the average per-query miss rate and is defined as follows

$$\overline{\text{pMiss}} = \frac{1}{|Q_r|} \sum_{q \in Q_r} \frac{\#\text{ misses of } q}{\#\text{ refs of } q} \qquad (2)$$

where Q_r is the set of queries with references in the data (i.e., each query has at least one relevant document). The number of references and the number of misses of query

---

[1] https://www.iarpa.gov/index.php/research-programs/material

q is computed based on the whole document collection $\mathcal{C}$ under consideration.

$\overline{\text{pFA}}$ is the average per-query false alarm rate and is defined as follows

$$\overline{\text{pFA}} = \frac{1}{|Q|} \sum_{q \in Q} \frac{\text{\# FAs of } q}{|\mathcal{C}| \text{ - \# refs of } q} \tag{3}$$

The constant β in Equation (1) reflects the relative importance of the two types of error.

One can also compute a per-query performance measure, the Query Weighted Value (QWV), defined for query q as

$$QWV = 1 - \text{pMiss}(q) - \beta\,\text{pFA}(q) \tag{4}$$

The AQWV metric has several important properties. The range is $(-\beta, 1]$, where a system that returns no detections would obtain a score of 0. It is possible for a system with a large number of false alarms to give a negative score. A correct detection for different queries is not weighted equally—the gain is related to the rarity of the query, as queries with fewer relevant documents gain more from each correct detection (e.g., think of the case where a query has only one truly relevant document, and, assuming no false alarms, accepting/rejecting that document will result in a QWV of one/zero). If we ignore the number of true references for a query in Equation 3—often this is reasonable as the number of documents dwarfs the number of true references—then there is a constant penalty for every false alarm. The constant β controls the strength of the penalty. All results in this paper use a β of 40, required by the evaluation task. This means the system has to be tuned to produce a very low false alarm rate: a single false alarm is penalized 40 times more than a single true miss. The general idea behind a high value of β is to minimize the amount of non-relevant documents the end user has to look through when using a CLIR system. The evaluation plan also suggests an effective CLIR system should reach an AQWV value of 0.5 or higher.

In the rest of the paper, we will denote by MQWV the maximum value that AQWV can attain by sweeping over all possible decision thresholds.

2.2. Data

The training dataset (Build set) consists of approximately 50 hours of audio (conversational telephone speech) for ASR and 800k words of bitext for MT. There are additional Dev and Analysis datasets drawn from the same data pool as the Evaluation dataset for internal testing and error analysis purpose.

Our system will be evaluated on the blind Evaluation dataset, which is not guaranteed to have the same query relevance probability as that of the Dev or Analysis dataset. Table 1 gives the size of each dataset we received. We also used existing additional speech and parallel text for building multilingual ASR and MT models. The detailed data used by each component will be covered in individual sections below.

2.3. Technical Approach

Figure 1 is a top-level block diagram of our CLIR and Summarization system. More details about the various compo-

Dataset	Lithuanian		Bulgarian	
	Text	Speech	Text	Speech
Build	610K	66 hr	735K	41 hr
Dev	174K	10 hr	202K	15 hr
Analysis	234K	10 hr	276K	18 hr
Evaluation	4.3M	172 hr	4.5M	183 hr

Table 1: Size of text (number of source tokens) and speech data provided in each language pack.

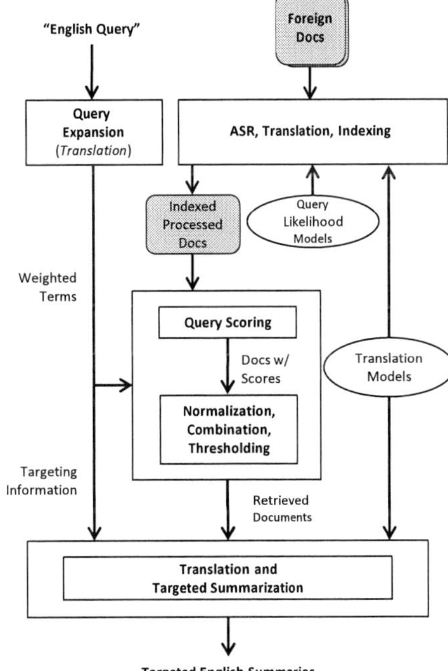

Figure 1: Block diagram of our CLIR and Summarization system

nents appear in Sections 5 and 6. At top right is an existing corpus of foreign audio and text documents, which go through ASR, translation and indexing steps. At top left, a user issues a query in English, which is then expanded through query expansion. Note term translations for CLIR can happen either after query expansion (from English to the foreign language) or in document precomputation (from the foreign language to English). Our preferred mode is to efficiently translate all terms in the foreign documents in all possible ways using the context of nearby words. Note that, given that documents have a longer context than queries, translation of documents to English is more precise than translation of short (nominally one-two words) English queries to the foreign language. The preprocessed data in the form of weighted search terms (from query expansion) and indexed documents serves as input to the CLIR query module, where each document receives a query relevance score. This is followed by score normalization, combination, and thresholding to maximize AQWV scores on the Dev or Analysis set. Finally, the retrieved documents, together with translation models and target information (where the CLIR evidence is from in the MT target), go through the Translation and Summarization module to produce final summary snippets in English.

3. Automatic Speech Recognition

3.1. Training Data

Our acoustic model is pretrained on approximately 1500 hours of narrowband conversational data from 11 languages (Keith et al., 2018). This pretrained multilingual model is then fine tuned to the target language. The fine tuning data consisted of the build_train and build_dev portions of the MATERIAL data. Note that, although the provided transcribed training speech is conversational telephone speech, the majority of the evaluation speech is wideband broadcast speech. So we also collected approximately 700 hours of untranscribed wideband data from YouTube in both Bulgarian and Lithuanian for semi-supervised training. We expand the acoustic training data by creating two additional copies that are augmented by noise, compression, and reverberation (Hartmann et al., 2016).

The language models are trained using four data sources: 1) acoustic transcripts, 2) build_bitext, 3) paracrawl (Esplà et al., 2019), 4) automatically collected web data. The procedure used to collect web data is described in (Zhang et al., 2015). A separate trigram language model is created for each data source and then interpolated to create a single language model.

3.2. Pronunciation Lexicon

We start with the original pronunciation lexicon provided with the build data. These pronunciations are also used to train a model using SequiturG2P (Bisani and Ney, 2008) in order to generate pronunciations for any additional words. Our final lexicon contains all words from the original build lexicon, the build_bitext, and the paracrawl data. We also include the most frequent 300k words in the web data. Combined, this brings the total number of words in the lexicon to approximately 400k.

3.3. Acoustic Model

We use a CNN-LSTM acoustic model. This model is similar to the TDNN-LSTM acoustic model, but with 8 convolutional layers prepended. In addition to the standard mel-filterbank features, we also include i-vectors for speaker adaptation. The Sage toolkit (Hsiao et al., 2016) is used for training and decoding with acoustic model training based on the Kaldi Chain model. Training consists of a single epoch using the LF-MMI criterion followed by an additional epoch using sMBR. After the supervised model is trained, we perform semi-supervised training. The original model is used to transcribe the collected YouTube data. We combine this automatically transcribed data with the original labeled data and retrain the model. Note that while both the supervised and unsupervised data are used during LF-MMI training, only the supervised data is used during sMBR training in order to limit the effects of errors in the unsupervised transcripts.

3.4. Language Model

We build both n-gram and RNN-based language models (LM). A trigram LM is constructed from each of the four sources of text data. The LMs are then interpolated with weights that minimize perplexity on the Analysis data. The RNN-LM is trained on the same set of data as described in (Xu et al., 2018). The neural model consists of two LSTM layers and three fully connected layers.

3.5. Decoding

All audio data is first decoded using the above described acoustic model with a trigram language model to generate initial lattices. The lattices are then rescored using the RNN-LM. The final step is to convert the rescored lattices into confusion networks (CNets).

4. Machine Translation

4.1. Training Data

The primary data source for constructing MT models is parallel data from the build language pack, augmented with a variety of web data, such as CommonCrawl[2] and open parallel corpus (Tiedemann, 2012). We used the PanLex dictionary (Kamholz et al., 2014) for the languages, simply by treating each translation as a (very short) parallel sentence. We also used parallel data from Russian and Ukrainian for building multilingual neural MT models. We employed an oversampling technique to ensure that the target languages (Lithuanian and Bulgarian) are well represented in the training. More specifically, we oversample data from each language with different oversampling factors so that the target language has a proportion of 70% in the final training data, while the other three languages have an equal proportion of 10% each. Table 2 summarizes the amount of training data used:

Language	Source Tokens (millions)
Lithuanian	13.1
Bulgarian	20.5
Russian	14.0
Ukrainian	9.7

Table 2: Amount of parallel data used in training multilingual MT models.

Our system needs to translate both the text data and the transcript from the ASR sub-system for use with summarization (Section 6). Because there is no casing information in the ASR transcript, we augmented the MT training data with the lower-cased version of the source data with punctuation marks removed to mimic the condition of ASR output. The neural MT models were trained on both versions of the data together, in a single "multi-style" fashion, to handle both text and ASR transcript as input. This was however not done for the phrase-based model described below.

---

[2]http://commoncrawl.org

4.2. MT Models

The machine translation component consists of two multi-lingual neural MT models and one phrase-based statistical MT (SMT) model:

1. Transformer NMT: a 6-layer transfomer-based model (Vaswani et al., 2017) jointly trained over Lithuanian, Bulgarian, Russian and Ukrainian data. We applied data oversampling and used 21k subword units in the vocabulary. We trained the model over the training data using 600k training steps with a batch size of 2048. We averaged the last 3 checkpoints to produce the final model.

2. DynamicConv NMT: a 6-layer dynamic convolution model (Wu et al., 2019) trained over the same data with 50k subword units. 1200k updates were used for the training. The final model was produced by model averaging of the last 3 checkpoints.

3. Moses Phrase-based SMT: a phrase-based statistical MT system trained over the Lithuanian or Bulgarian bilingual data.

All MT models produce N-best (N=20) hypotheses as output for downstream summarization processing. We used the tensor2tensor toolkit (Vaswani et al., 2018) for the transformer implementation and the fairseq toolkit (Ott et al., 2019) for the dynamic convolution model. We also used Moses (Koehn et al., 2007) for training the phrase-based model. Our own tokenizer was used instead of the tokenizer from Moses to match the tokenization scheme used by other system components. Subword tokenization was done using the sentencepiece toolkit (Kudo and Richardson, 2018), an unsupervised text tokenization method that is independent of the language being processed.

5. CLIR

The CLIR system consists of a number of components for performing indexing, query processing, retrieval, score normalization, system combination, and thresholding. These components are described in more detail below.

5.1. Query Processing

We treat queries in two distinct ways: (i) as *flat strings*, where the query words are used as a "bag of words", completely ignoring the context-free nature of the queries; this is the mode used in the paper (Zbib et al., 2019); (ii) as *hierarchical*, expressed using a parse tree, where the MATERIAL-provided context-free grammar (CFG) is used for this purpose. The leaves of the tree correspond to individual terms, while internal nodes of the tree correspond to various query types such as *LEXICAL PHRASE, PLUS, EXAMPLE_OF*, etc.

In the case of the *flat* query treatment, we consider query translation (to the foreign language) as well as document translation (to English) as two distinct modes of retrieval.

In the case of the *parse tree*, PLUS and EXAMPLE_OF (CONCEPTUAL) query components are further *expanded* to include additional query terms that are used in the search. Specifically, the terms of the PLUS components are expanded using nearest-neighbor words of English pre-trained Wikipedia-derived word embeddings (Bojanowski et al., 2017) (with a minimum cosine similarity $\cos_{\min}$, typically between 0.3-0.4). The weight of each expansion is an exponential function of the cosine similarity, as follows

$$w = \exp\{-\alpha(1 - \cos)/(1 - \cos_{\min})\} \qquad (5)$$

where α is a tunable coefficient (typically equal to 3.0 in our experiments). This weight is multiplied with the probability of occurrence of the term in the document. The terms of the EXAMPLE_OF components are expanded using both WordNet and pre-trained monolingual embeddings as follows:

- Pre-Processing: Find all senses of the EXAMPLE_OF argument phrase in WordNet as NLTK Synset objects.

- WordNet Hyponym Traversal: For each Synset, recursively traverse its hyponym tree and record all hyponyms found during the process.

- Post-Processing: Filter out any hyponyms that have a vector cosine distance relative to the original EXAMPLE_OF phrase greater than 0.35. As above, we use the word embeddings from (Bojanowski et al., 2017).

For instance, the expansions for the query EXAMPLE_OF(footwear) include: "baby shoe", "bowling shoe", "sneaker", "wooden shoe", "rubber boot", "congress shoe", "ghillie", "combat boot", "footgear", "huarache", etc.

5.2. Indexing

We construct inverted indexes for both the source language and the target language. For text documents, we index words and n-grams. For speech documents, we index both the 1-best output (which is treated as regular text) and the confusion network, saving the ASR posterior score. The index contains the location of the words and the n-grams as well as the probability of translation to the target (query) language, scaled by the ASR posterior in the case of speech. The probability of translation is obtained from the GIZA translation table (generating GIZA alignments is usually one of the first steps run in a MT system), interpolated with the Neural Network Lexical Translation Model (NNLTM) score. More details about NNLTM can be found in (Zbib et al., 2019). Note that the indexing is done with both original and stemmed English words.

5.3. Retrieval Models

The individual retrieval models are as follows:

- For "flat" queries, four retrievals are performed: with original/stemmed words and with document/query translation. (Obviously, the appropriate index is used in each case.) For the case of document translation, two confidence score computations are also done: using the simple probabilistic model and with the probability of occurrence (see (Zbib et al., 2019) for details).

- For "hierarchical" queries, the parse tree is used as a "processing tree", akin to an *abstract syntax tree* used in computer language compilers. Then, the process of retrieval can be accomplished using a depth-first traversal of the tree. Terminal nodes compute the locations where individual query words (original or expanded) are matched in a document, based on what is in the inverted index. Internal (non-terminal) nodes of the tree perform an operation corresponding to the query type: e.g., for PLUS or EXAMPLE_OF queries, the individual retrievals of the "children" nodes (query terms or expanded terms) are combined using a probability of occurrence operation. Similarly, an internal node that corresponds to a LEXICAL PHRASE only keeps retrievals that are "close" to each other and penalizes for missing phrase words.

- Whole-phrase matching, where, if a phrase query component existed in the phrase translation table, and if the source phrase translation existed in the document, the corresponding probability was used in the retrieval.

- In all cases above, two retrievals are done in the case of Speech: using ASR 1-best and ASR confusion networks (cnets). While the cnets provide better performance, the 1-best helps in combination.

5.4. Normalization, Combination, and Thresholding

The detection scores of each of the individual systems are normalized using a learned model. The model computes a linear combination of the following features:

1. Original retrieval $score(q, d)$ for query q and document d

2. The QST-transformed score $score_{\text{qst}}(q, d)$, where QST is a technique similar to KST, described in (Karakos et al., 2013)

3. The normalized sum $\sum_{d \in \mathcal{C}} score(q, d)/|\mathcal{C}|$

4. The three features:

$$\min_{w \in q}\{score(w, d)\}, \ \max_{w \in q}\{score(w, d)\}, \ \operatorname{avg}_{w \in q}\{score(w, d)\},$$

   where avg_w is just the average over all words w in query q (esp. for multi-word queries).

5. The three features:

$$\min_{w \in q}\{\operatorname{count}(w)\}, \ \max_{w \in q}\{\operatorname{count}(w)\}, \ \operatorname{avg}_{w \in q}\{\operatorname{count}(w)\},$$

   where $\operatorname{count}(w)$ is the count of w in the IR training data (e.g., parallel data used to train the bilingual dictionary for CLIR).

The weights in the linear combination are computed using Powell's method (Karakos et al., 2013), with the objective to maximize MQWV.

Combination of a subset of the individual systems (determined through performance on Analysis and Dev) is done by interpolating the log probabilities from the different systems, with weights determined using Powell's method, as mentioned above.

The final output on the test set is thresholded by tuning the overall proportion of accepted documents according to performance of the query set on the Analysis document set.

5.5. Evidence for Summarization

Besides outputting scores and decisions for all documents that have been accepted, the CLIR system outputs an evidence "object" for each sentence that has a nonzero score for a query. The evidence object specifies the source segment, source word, query word found, and the probability for that query word. These evidence objects are just referred to as "evidence" in the summarization section below.

6. Summarization

6.1. Overview

The task of the summarization component is to create English-language summaries for the documents that are retrieved by the CLIR component. The summarization component makes use of query "evidence" provided by CLIR component and English translations provided by the MT component to rank and select appropriate sentences (or fixed-length snippets) in order to form a summary that can be presented to human users. Below we describe in more detail, the mechanism to use output from CLIR and MT components, our extractive selection algorithm, and some presentation aspects of the summarization component.

6.2. Combining Output from Multiple CLIR Systems

As explained above, the CLIR component is comprised of multiple systems that each produce their individual output. While the system combination step in CLIR takes care of combining the relevance decision and document-level relevance scores output by these systems, the word-level evidence information is combined by the summarization component. This combined information is then used in the sentence selection process (described below). The word-level evidence provides, for every query word likely to appear in a sentence, the probability of its occurrence. This probability is derived by interpolation of GIZA and NNLTM translation probabilities. The summarization component uses a weighted sum of these probabilities to form an aggregate score for a query word appearing in a sentence.

6.3. Combining Output from Multiple MT Systems

The summarization component uses top-K English sentences from the nbest output of each of the three MT systems–Transformer, DynamicConv, and Moses. For the evaluation, the value of K was set to 4. Summarization component looks for specific query words within these sentences based on the evidence provided by CLIR and also a direct string match. It then creates fix-sized snippets around these query words. These snippets are then used for ranking and selection to form the final summary.

Note that the summarization component has the ability to extract either full sentences or fix-sized snippets in order

Language	Text			Speech			All
	AQWV	pMiss	pFA	AQWV	pMiss	pFA	AQWV
Lithuanian	0.617	0.287	0.002	0.609	0.306	0.002	**0.613**
Bulgarian	0.695	0.186	0.003	0.654	0.210	0.003	**0.675**

Table 3: Official AQWV scores for Text and Speech data on the evaluation set with a β of 40. The All column reports a single AQWV system score computed as the mean of the Text and Speech AQWV scores.

to create the summary. For the evaluation, we chose to use fix-sized snippets that extend up to 7 words before and after the query word.

6.4. Snippet Selection Algorithm

Our extractive snippet selection algorithm is a submodular selection algorithm that uses both query-evidence and tf-idf scores in its coverage and diversity objectives (Lin and Bilmes, 2011). The query words that are discovered by direct string match, and that for some reason were not captured in interpolated GIZA-NNLTM translation tables, are assigned a fixed score. It is also worth mentioning that we do some special handling for expanded queries. For expanded queries, we use a cutoff on the list of expanded query terms, so as to reduce possible noise in summary output and also lower the computation time needed for snippet-selection itself. We experimented with various cutoffs and found that a cutoff of 3 worked best for text summaries, while a cutoff of 0 (no expanded terms) worked best for audio summaries.

We select the top two snippets ranked by the submodular algorithm to form the final summary, which in part is motivated by (Maxwell et al., 2017), who show that for a summarization system for IR, longer summaries are not necessarily beneficial for human-in-the-loop relevance judgments. Since we use nbest English sentences from multiple MT systems, there is a possibility (although bleak) that some adjacently ranked snippets can have a large information overlap. To address that, after selecting a snippet from a given unique sentence (based on the mapping sentence ID from the foreign language side), we preclude other snippets from that sentence from the selection process.

6.5. Presentation Aspects of Summaries

Based on the presentation scheme used by (Boschee et al., 2019b), our summaries have the query words (or any word that is likely to be an alternative translation for the query word) highlighted in blue. A footnote is also attached to each highlighted word, which is composed of the alternative translations that the highlighted word could have in the context. These alternative translations are the top 5 words appearing in a combined GIZA-NNLTM interpolated translation table, where the combined table is created by applying Borda ranking[3] to multiple GIZA-NNLTM interpolation tables used by various CLIR systems. See figure 2 for a sample summary from the Lithuanian system.

7. Results

Table 3 gives the official AQWV scores for Lithuanian and Bulgarian on Text and Speech conditions of the evaluation

Figure 2: Sample summary snippet returned from the Lithuanian system for a plus query "car accident victim"+

data. A β of 40 is used to penalize false alarms when computing AQWV scores. Consequently our system is tuned to produce a very low probability of the average per-query false alarm ($\overline{\text{pFA}}$) at the cost of relatively high probability of miss ($\overline{\text{pMiss}}$).

In addition to the AQWV results on the evaluation set, we also present results from our ASR and MT components on the Analysis set where we have references. In table 4 we give the word error rate (WER) and BLEU scores our system produced on the Analysis sets. The BLEU scores are obtained using the `mteval-v11b` scoring script from NIST.[4] For the MT result, the two neural MT models, transformer (NMT-T) and dynamic convolution (NMT-D), have similar performance, and are much better than that from the SMT Moses system. The gain of the NMT over SMT model is largely due to multilingual training, which is not possible with the phrase based SMT. Because sometimes our Summarization component will choose the rendering of a snippet from the SMT instead of that from the neural MT system, we decide to include SMT as part of the translation pipeline.

Language	WER	BLEU		
MT Model		NMT-T	NMT-D	SMT
Lithuanian	18.7	30.4	30.5	20.0
Bulgarian	17.6	43.8	43.5	34.7

Table 4: WER and BLEU scores for Lithuanian and Bulgarian on the Analysis set.

8. Low-Resource Languages

In this paper, we only reported experimental results from two medium-resource languages as part of the October 2019 MATERIAL evaluation. However, all the techniques discussed in this paper are applicable to low-resource languages. Since such languages have very limited training data, techniques such as semi-supervised training, can be

---

[3]http://en.wikipedia.org/wiki/Borda_count

[4]https://www.nist.gov/itl/iad/mig/tools

employed to leverage large amounts of existing or web collected data to further improve system performance. This can be done for speech recognition or machine translation via back translation (Sennrich et al., 2016). Previously, we had applied our system to low-resource languages such as Somali, Swahili, and Tagalog. More recently, we applied our system to Pashto as part of the MATERIAL Surprise language Sprint in early 2020 and achieved very good performance.

9. Summary

In this paper, we presented a CLIR system that can perform information retrieval over audio and text documents from a foreign language and present summaries in English. Key features of our system include an appropriate probabilistic CLIR model that uses a neural network lexical translation model, strong multilingual neural speech recognition and neural translation models, plus advanced score normalization, combination, and thresholding schemes. Furthermore, our system is language agnostic and can be quickly brought up for a new low-resource language in a few days. In the future, we plan to explore better ways of using harvested data to enhance CLIR, ASR, and MT in the form of semi-supervised training.

10. Acknowledgements

This work was supported by the Intelligence Advanced Research Projects Activity (IARPA) via Department of Defense US Air Force Research Laboratory contract number FA8650-17-C-9118.

11. Bibliographical References

Bisani, M. and Ney, H. (2008). Joint-sequence models for grapheme-to-phoneme conversion. *Speech Communication*, 50(5):434 – 451.

Bojanowski, P., Grave, E., Joulin, A., and Mikolov, T. (2017). Enriching word vectors with subword information. *Transactions of the Association for Computational Linguistics*, 5:135–146.

Boschee, E., Barry, J., Billa, J., Freedman, M., Gowda, T., Lignos, C., Palen-Michel, C., Pust, M., Khonglah, B. K., Madikeri, S., May, J., and Miller, S. (2019a). SARAL: A low-resource cross-lingual domain-focused information retrieval system for effective rapid document triage. In Marta R. Costa-jussà et al., editors, *Proceedings of the 57th Conference of the Association for Computational Linguistics, ACL 2019, Florence, Italy, July 28 - August 2, 2019, Volume 3: System Demonstrations*, pages 19–24. Association for Computational Linguistics.

Boschee, E., Barry, J., Billa, J., Freedman, M., Gowda, T., Lignos, C., Palen-Michel, C., Pust, M., Khonglah, B. K., Madikeri, S., May, J., and Miller, S. (2019b). SARAL: A low-resource cross-lingual domain-focused information retrieval system for effective rapid document triage. In *Proceedings of the 57th Annual Meeting of the Association for Computational Linguistics: System Demonstrations*, pages 19–24, Florence, Italy, July. Association for Computational Linguistics.

Esplà, M., Forcada, M., Ramírez-Sánchez, G., and Hoang, H. (2019). ParaCrawl: Web-scale parallel corpora for the languages of the EU. In *Proceedings of Machine Translation Summit XVII Volume 2: Translator, Project and User Tracks*, pages 118–119, Dublin, Ireland, August. European Association for Machine Translation.

Hartmann, W., Ng, T., Hsiao, R., Tsakalidis, S., and Schwartz, R. M. (2016). Two-stage data augmentation for low-resourced speech recognition. In Nelson Morgan, editor, *Interspeech 2016, 17th Annual Conference of the International Speech Communication Association, San Francisco, CA, USA, September 8-12, 2016*, pages 2378–2382. ISCA.

Hsiao, R., Meermeier, R., Ng, T., Huang, Z., Jordan, M., Kan, E., Alumäe, T., Silovský, J., Hartmann, W., Keith, F., Lang, O., Siu, M., and Kimball, O. (2016). Sage: The new BBN speech processing platform. In Nelson Morgan, editor, *Interspeech 2016, 17th Annual Conference of the International Speech Communication Association, San Francisco, CA, USA, September 8-12, 2016*, pages 3022–3026. ISCA.

Kamholz, D., Pool, J., and Colowick, S. M. (2014). Panlex: Building a resource for panlingual lexical translation. In *Proceedings of the Ninth International Conference on Language Resources and Evaluation, LREC 2014, Reykjavik, Iceland, May 26-31, 2014*, pages 3145–3150.

Karakos, D., Schwartz, R. M., Tsakalidis, S., Zhang, L., Ranjan, S., Ng, T., Hsiao, R., Saikumar, G., Bulyko, I., Nguyen, L., Makhoul, J., Grézl, F., Hannemann, M., Karafiát, M., Szöke, I., Veselý, K., Lamel, L., and Le, V. B. (2013). Score normalization and system combination for improved keyword spotting. In *2013 IEEE Workshop on Automatic Speech Recognition and Understanding, Olomouc, Czech Republic, December 8-12, 2013*, pages 210–215. IEEE.

Keith, F., Hartmann, W., Siu, M., Ma, J. Z., and Kimball, O. (2018). Optimizing multilingual knowledge transfer for time-delay neural networks with low-rank factorization. In *2018 IEEE International Conference on Acoustics, Speech and Signal Processing, ICASSP 2018, Calgary, AB, Canada, April 15-20, 2018*, pages 4924–4928. IEEE.

Koehn, P., Hoang, H., Birch, A., Callison-Burch, C., Federico, M., Bertoldi, N., Cowan, B., Shen, W., Moran, C., Zens, R., Dyer, C., Bojar, O., Constantin, A., and Herbst, E. (2007). Moses: Open source toolkit for statistical machine translation. In *ACL 2007, Proceedings of the 45th Annual Meeting of the Association for Computational Linguistics, June 23-30, 2007, Prague, Czech Republic*.

Kudo, T. and Richardson, J. (2018). Sentencepiece: A simple and language independent subword tokenizer and detokenizer for neural text processing. In *Proceedings of the 2018 Conference on Empirical Methods in Natural Language Processing, EMNLP 2018: System Demonstrations, Brussels, Belgium, October 31 - November 4, 2018*, pages 66–71.

Lin, H. and Bilmes, J. (2011). A class of submodular functions for document summarization. In *Proceedings of the 49th Annual Meeting of the Association for Computational Linguistics: Human Language Technologies*, pages 510–520.

Maxwell, D., Azzopardi, L., and Moshfeghi, Y. (2017). A study of snippet length and informativeness: Behaviour, performance and user experience. In *Proceedings of the 40th International ACM SIGIR Conference on Research and Development in Information Retrieval*, SIGIR '17, pages 135–144, New York, NY, USA. Association for Computing Machinery.

Ott, M., Edunov, S., Baevski, A., Fan, A., Gross, S., Ng, N., Grangier, D., and Auli, M. (2019). fairseq: A fast, extensible toolkit for sequence modeling. In *Proceedings of NAACL-HLT 2019: Demonstrations*.

Sennrich, R., Haddow, B., and Birch, A. (2016). Improving neural machine translation models with monolingual data. In *Proceedings of the 54th Annual Meeting of the Association for Computational Linguistics, ACL 2016, August 7-12, 2016, Berlin, Germany, Volume 1: Long Papers*. The Association for Computer Linguistics.

Tiedemann, J. (2012). Parallel data, tools and interfaces in OPUS. In *Proceedings of the Eighth International Conference on Language Resources and Evaluation, LREC 2012, Istanbul, Turkey, May 23-25, 2012*, pages 2214–2218.

Vaswani, A., Shazeer, N., Parmar, N., Uszkoreit, J., Jones, L., Gomez, A. N., Kaiser, L., and Polosukhin, I. (2017). Attention is all you need. In *Advances in Neural Information Processing Systems 30: Annual Conference on Neural Information Processing Systems 2017, 4-9 December 2017, Long Beach, CA, USA*, pages 5998–6008.

Vaswani, A., Bengio, S., Brevdo, E., Chollet, F., Gomez, A. N., Gouws, S., Jones, L., Kaiser, L., Kalchbrenner, N., Parmar, N., Sepassi, R., Shazeer, N., and Uszkoreit, J. (2018). Tensor2tensor for neural machine translation. In *Proceedings of the 13th Conference of the Association for Machine Translation in the Americas, AMTA 2018, Boston, MA, USA, March 17-21, 2018 - Volume 1: Research Papers*, pages 193–199.

Wu, F., Fan, A., Baevski, A., Dauphin, Y., and Auli, M. (2019). Pay less attention with lightweight and dynamic convolutions. In *International Conference on Learning Representations*.

Xu, H., Chen, T., Gao, D., Wang, Y., Li, K., Goel, N., Carmiel, Y., Povey, D., and Khudanpur, S. (2018). A pruned rnnlm lattice-rescoring algorithm for automatic speech recognition. In *2018 IEEE International Conference on Acoustics, Speech and Signal Processing, ICASSP 2018, Calgary, AB, Canada, April 15-20, 2018*, pages 5929–5933. IEEE.

Zbib, R., Zhao, L., Karakos, D., Hartmann, W., DeYoung, J., Huang, Z., Jiang, Z., Rivkin, N., Zhang, L., Schwartz, R. M., and Makhoul, J. (2019). Neural-network lexical translation for cross-lingual IR from text and speech. In Benjamin Piwowarski, et al., editors, *Proceedings of the 42nd International ACM SIGIR Conference on Research and Development in Information Retrieval, SIGIR 2019, Paris, France, July 21-25, 2019*, pages 645–654. ACM.

Zhang, L., Karakos, D., Hartmann, W., Hsiao, R., Schwartz, R. M., and Tsakalidis, S. (2015). Enhancing low resource keyword spotting with automatically retrieved web documents. In *INTERSPEECH 2015, 16th Annual Conference of the International Speech Communication Association, Dresden, Germany, September 6-10, 2015*, pages 839–843. ISCA.

Proceedings of the Cross-Language Search and Summarization of Text and Speech Workshop, pages 52–57
Language Resources and Evaluation Conference (LREC 2020), Marseille, 11–16 May 2020
© European Language Resources Association (ELRA), licensed under CC-BY-NC

What Set of Documents to Present to an Analyst?

Richard Schwartz, John Makhoul, Lee Tarlin, Damianos Karakos
Raytheon BBN Technologies
Cambridge MA, USA
{rich.schwartz,john.makhoul,lee.tarlin,damianos.karakos}@raytheon.com

Abstract

We describe the human triage scenario envisioned in the Cross-Lingual Information Retrieval (CLIR) problem of the IARPA MATE-RIAL Program. The overall goal is to maximize the quality of the set of documents that is given to a bilingual analyst, as measured by the *AQWV* score. The initial set of source documents that are retrieved by the CLIR system is summarized in English and presented to human judges who attempt to remove the irrelevant documents (false alarms); the resulting documents are then presented to the analyst. First, we describe the *AQWV* performance measure and show that, in our experience, if the acceptance threshold of the CLIR component has been optimized to maximize *AQWV*, the loss in *AQWV* due to false alarms is relatively constant across many conditions, which also limits the possible gain that can be achieved by any post filter (such as human judgments) that removes false alarms. Second, we analyze the likely benefits for the triage operation as a function of the initial CLIR *AQWV* score and the ability of the human judges to remove false alarms without removing relevant documents. Third, we demonstrate that we can increase the benefit for human judgments by combining the human judgment scores with the original document scores returned by the automatic CLIR system.

Keywords: cross-lingual information retrieval, average query weighted value, AQWV

1. Introduction

The goal of the IARPA MATERIAL[1] Program is to search a corpus of foreign language documents and to return those documents that are relevant to an English language query in order to give those documents to a bilingual analyst. The program envisions a two-stage procedure. The first stage uses an automatic CLIR system that takes a structured English query and retrieves foreign documents that are likely to be relevant to that query.

However, there is usually a shortage of qualified bilingual analysts. So we would like to do anything we can to reduce the number of false alarms in the returned lists. The solution in the MATERIAL program is a second stage, which is a triage operation in which the system produces a short English summary for each of the returned documents, that provides the evidence for the document being relevant to the query. These summaries are shown to an English-speaking triage analyst whose job is to discard documents that they believe might be irrelevant. In fact, rather than making a binary decision, the analyst is asked to provide a judgment score from 1 to 5 reflecting how likely they think it is that the document is relevant.

In the next section, we will describe the AQWV measure and explain why this measure might be appropriate for this particular task. We compare it with the Mean Average Precision (MAP) measure that is most commonly used for measuring IR performance (Manning et al., 2008).

In section 3, we look at the maximum possible benefit that could be achieved by perfect triage judgments – judgments that discard all of the irrelevant documents without discarding any relevant documents. We show, empirically, that when the acceptance threshold for a system is optimized to maximize AQWV, the loss due to false alarms is relatively constant and fairly small (approximately 10%), across a wide range of conditions. And we also show that this is not true for the MAP measure. Of course, the Triage an-

alysts cannot do this job perfectly, so we look at the theoretical performance that can be achieved, given that the average triage analyst has some probability of correctly rejecting an irrelevant document (TR) and another probability of falsely rejecting a relevant document (FR). We will show that the triage analyst has a very difficult task, especially if the initial performance of the automatic CLIR system is very good.

In Section 4, we examine the results of actual experiments and we measure the improvement that we get by setting a threshold on the judgment scores produced by the triage analysts. In Section 5, we consider better ways to use the triage analysts' judgments. In particular, we show that it is advantageous to combine the triage judgment score for a document with the original CLIR score before comparing with any threshold. This makes it more likely that the triage judgments can improve the quality of the documents provided to the final bilingual analyst.

2. The AQWV Measure

In some applications (such as web searches), the search engine returns a ranked list of documents and the user may look at as many documents as they need until they find the information they want. So it is particularly important that the most relevant documents are near the beginning of the list. In contrast, in the application here, we assume that the user is not just looking for a "good enough relevant document". Instead, they would like to find *all* relevant documents. But at the same time, they cannot afford to look at too many irrelevant documents. So instead of returning a ranked list of documents, the system will return a truncated list of documents and the analyst will read all of them.

To reflect this different need, the performance measure used is the Average Query Weighted Value (AQWV). For each query, we measure the recall and the false alarm performance. The *recall* $= (1 - pMiss)$ is the fraction of all of the relevant documents that were included in the returned list. The false alarm rate, *pFA*, is the fraction of the non-relevant

---

[1] https://www.iarpa.gov/index.php/research-programs/material

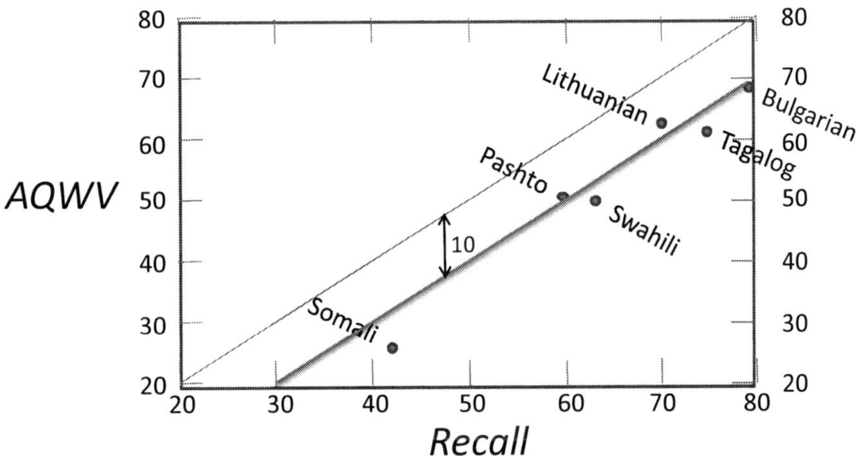

Figure 1: The AQWV vs. Recall values for 6 MATERIAL languages. The upper diagonal line represents *AQWV = Recall*. The lower diagonal line represents *AQWV = Recall – 10*. Most languages fall near the lower line.

documents in the corpus that show up in the returned list. Note that, while *pMiss* might be in the range from 20% to 80%, *pFA* is likely to be a small number, since the number of documents in the corpus is large.

The performance for a single query, or *QWV* is simply a weighted combination of these two measures:

$$QWV_q = 1 - pMiss_q - \beta \times pFA_q \qquad (1)$$

$$QWV_q = Recall_q - \beta \times pFA_q \qquad (2)$$

where β is a weight that reflects the relative cost of giving false alarms to the analyst and is usually $>> 1$ because *pFA* is usually much smaller than *pMiss*. In most of our experiments, $\beta = 40$.

The overall score for a set of queries, *AQWV*, is simply the average of the *QWV* for all of the queries.

$$AQWV = Avg_q[QWV_q] \qquad (3)$$

However, it is possible that some of the queries might actually have no relevant documents in the corpus being searched, so we cannot compute *Recall* for those queries. At the same time, any irrelevant documents returned (false alarms) in response to those queries are still costly. So we change the computation such that we only compute the average *Recall* on those queries that have relevant documents, while the average *pFA* is computed over all queries.

$$AQWV = Avg_{q-rel}[Recall_q] - \beta \times Avg_{all-q}[pFA_q] \quad (4)$$

The measure that is more commonly used in Information Retrieval (IR) research is the Mean Average Precision (MAP). We assume, here, that the ranked list of documents produced by a system using AQWV and MAP are the same. However, the system does not have the option of changing the number of documents returned for each query. It is a constant number, for example 100. Of course, the goal is to return as many of the relevant documents as possible within that list, but also to rank them such that the relevant documents are as close to the beginning of the list as possible. For each query, we compute the precision at the rank of each relevant document. Any document that is not in the retrieved list is given a precision of zero. Then, we average the precision values over the relevant documents. (Hence the name "Average Precision".) So the main difference is that with AQWV, we have the opportunity to vary the length of the list in order to reduce the number of irrelevant documents retrieved for any given query.

3. Possible Benefit for Triage Judgments

We measured the cost of the false alarms ($\beta \times pFA$) over several languages with very different performance. We also measured the benefit for different values of β. One might think that when the cost for false alarms (β) is higher, the possible benefit for triage judgments is larger. In fact, this is not the case.

If the triage judges were perfect, the *AQWV* after the triage would be equal to the Recall for that system. Figure 1 shows the *AQWV* as a function of the *Recall* for six MATERIAL languages with a wide range of *AQWV* and *Recall*. It is worth noting that the value of β was not the same for all of these languages. β was 20 for Swahili and Tagalog, and 40 for the other four languages. But still, we see that the loss for false alarms is roughly the same (actually slightly more for Swahili and Tagalog, even though the cost for each false alarm was smaller). The upper diagonal line shows *AQWV = Recall*. The lower diagonal line shows *AQWV = Recall*–10. As can be seen, most of the languages fall very close to the lower line, with losses due to false alarms of 8% to 13% absolute. The loss due to false alarms represents the maximum possible benefit for removing false alarms. We have made similar measurements with different values of β and the results are always the same. When β increases and the system is tuned to choose the optimal threshold, it automatically produces

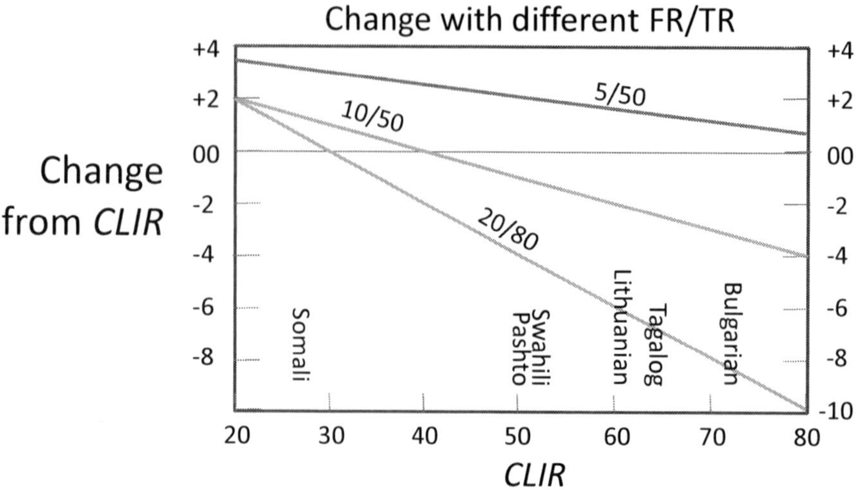

Figure 2: A plot of the expected change in *AQWV* that would accompany a Triage operation with the specified FR/TR (False Rejection / True Rejection) behavior, as a function of the initial *AQWV* produced by the CLIR system. For reference, we show the initial *CLIR* for 6 languages.

fewer false alarms and in doing so, it also decreases recall. Empirically, we find that the resulting loss for false alarms is always about the same. In the Babel program for keyword spotting we used the ATWV measure (Karakos et al., 2013; Alumäe et al., 2017), which is analogous to the AQWV measure. We found this same result for 26 different languages. So it seems to be an empirical property of the measure.

It might seem surprising that maximum possible cost of the false alarms is both relatively constant and also fairly small. This is not typically true with other measures, like MAP. The reason is that, with MAP, the system does not have the opportunity (or any incentive) to reduce the number of false alarms by reducing the number of documents retrieved. If it did reduce the returned documents, the only possible effect would be to replace the precision for some of the retrieved documents with a precision of zero, which is always worse. Let us consider the case of a representative ranked list. Typically, the ranked list has more relevant documents near the head of the list and the relevant documents are more sparse as we go down the list. Let us consider a query with 10 relevant documents and assume that the relevant documents occur at every power of 2. So the relevant documents are at rank 1, 2, 4, 8, ...512. Only 7 of these 10 documents would appear within the first 100 returned documents. When we compute the average precision at each of these ranks, we get a list of 10 precisions: 1, 1, 3/4, 4/8, 5/16, 6/32, 7/64, 0, 0, 0. The average of these numbers is .3859375 or 38.6%. Let's say we had a person who could review all of the 100 retrieved documents and correctly remove all of the irrelevant documents. In this case, the precision for the 7 documents within the list would be 1, so the overall precision would be 0.7 or 70%, which is a very large improvement. But the cost for this improvement would be very large because it would require that the person review 93 false documents. The *AQWV* measure is an attempt to include the

cost of that review.

But why is it that, when we optimize the threshold or the number of retrieved documents, the cost of the remaining false alarms is always around 10%? There is certainly no proof that this must be the case, because it depends on the distribution of the relevant documents. But let us consider a distribution of relevant documents similar to the one described above. That is, we assume that at any given rank, the number of relevant documents within that rank, R is $\log_2(R) + 1$. So at rank 8, we would have 4 relevant documents, just as in the example above.

In Table 1 below, we show the *AQWV* as a function of the number of documents retained (in the left column) and the value of *Beta*. The second column shows the expected recall for each number of retrieved documents, which is just the number of retrieved documents divided by 10. We assume there are 10,000 documents in the entire corpus. For each number of retrieved documents and value of *Beta*, we give the value of *AQWV*. The optimal *AQWV* (in this quantized table) and any value within 0.004 of this best value is shown in **bold**. For *Beta=10*, the cost of false alarms is very low. So the best result shown is if we retrieve 120 to 140 documents. We see that the recall is between 79% and 81% and the *AQWV* is 68% - about 11% to 13% worse. When *Beta* increases, the best *AQWV* is achieved with fewer retrieved documents, because the cost of false alarms is not worth the sparse relevant documents with larger lists. As can be seen, in each case, the difference between the optimal *AQWV* and the recall at that same list size is between 0.1 and 0.13, or 10% to 13%. We suspect that this will be the case for most functions where the relevant documents become more sparse as we go further down the list. Of course, for any single query, this may not be the case, but when we average over many queries it will always tend to be true.

From our empirical results with different languages and

List-Size	Recall	Beta									
L	$\log_2(L)+1$	10	20	30	40	50	60	70	80	90	100
10	0.432	0.427	0.421	0.415	0.410	0.404	0.398	0.392	0.387	0.381	0.375
15	0.491	0.481	0.471	0.460	0.450	0.440	0.430	0.420	0.410	**0.400**	**0.390**
20	0.532	0.518	0.503	0.488	0.474	0.459	**0.444**	**0.429**	**0.415**	**0.400**	0.385
25	0.564	0.545	0.526	0.506	0.487	**0.468**	**0.448**	**0.429**	0.410	0.390	0.371
30	0.591	0.567	0.543	0.518	**0.494**	**0.470**	0.446	0.422	0.398	0.374	0.350
40	0.632	0.599	0.565	**0.531**	**0.498**	0.464	0.430	0.396	0.363	0.329	0.295
50	0.664	0.621	0.578	**0.534**	0.491	0.448	0.404	0.361	0.318	0.274	0.231
60	0.691	0.638	**0.585**	0.531	0.478	0.425	0.372	0.319	0.266	0.213	0.160
70	0.713	0.650	**0.587**	0.524	0.461	0.399	0.336	0.273	0.210	0.147	0.084
80	0.732	0.660	**0.587**	0.514	0.442	0.369	0.296	0.223	0.151	0.078	0.005
90	0.749	0.667	0.584	0.502	0.419	0.337	0.254	0.172	0.089	0.007	-0.076
100	0.764	0.672	0.580	0.487	0.395	0.303	0.210	0.118	0.026	-0.067	-0.159
110	0.778	0.676	0.574	0.472	0.369	0.267	0.165	0.063	-0.040	-0.142	-0.244
120	0.791	**0.679**	0.567	0.454	0.342	0.230	0.118	0.006	-0.106	-0.218	-0.330
130	0.802	**0.680**	0.558	0.436	0.314	0.192	0.070	-0.052	-0.174	-0.296	-0.418
140	0.813	**0.681**	0.549	0.417	0.285	0.154	0.022	-0.110	-0.242	-0.374	-0.506

Table 1: AQWV scores as a function of list size and Beta value for a corpus of 10,000 documents. The optimal value of AQWV in each column is in bold. The difference between this value and the recall in the second column is usually between 0.1 and 0.13.

conditions, we believe that the maximum we can benefit from removing irrelevant documents is approximately 10% absolute. But of course, real triage judgments will not achieve this benefit because there will be some false rejection of relevant documents and false acceptance of irrelevant documents. Below, we derive the benefit that can be achieved for a system as a function of the initial *AQWV*. First, we define the cost of false alarms, *cFA*. We denote *CLIR* as a shorthand for the *AQWV* that results from the CLIR system.

$$cFA = \beta \times pFA \qquad (5)$$

$$CLIR = Recall - cFA \qquad (6)$$

$$Recall = CLIR + cFA \qquad (7)$$

Now after rejecting some documents through Triage judgments, we can define the percentage of true rejections, TR, and the percentage of false rejections, FR. Define *Triage* as the *AQWV* that results after removing those documents. So by correctly removing false alarms, *Triage* will go up by $TR \times cFA$. On the other hand, but removing relevant documents, *Triage* will go down by $FR \times Recall$. So the resulting Triage score will be

$$Triage = CLIR + TR \times cFA - FR \times Recall \qquad (8)$$

And substituting *Recall* from the preceding equation, the change in *AQWV* from the Triage process will be

$$Change = Triage - CLIR$$
$$= TR \times cFA - FR \times (CLIR + cFA)$$

We can plot $Change$ as a function of the original CLIR score for Triage systems with different FR/TR behavior.

In the Figure 2, we assume that *cFA* = 10%, because this is the typical behavior.

For example, a good Triage system (good summaries and good judges) might result in only 10% FR, together with 50% TR. That is, the triage analyst removes half of the false alarms, at a cost of losing only 10% of the relevant documents returned by the CLIR. As can be seen in the figure, as the initial *AQWV* increases, the change in *AQWV* decreases and is usually negative rather than positive. There is only a small predicted gain of about 1% absolute for the lowest initial *AQWV* (on Somali). For the other languages, there are substantial losses rather than the gain hoped for. A different summarization system and set of triage judges might have a different operating point, where they are able to correctly reject 80% of the irrelevant documents, but at a cost of falsely rejecting 20% of the relevant documents. While one might predict that this system might have similar overall performance, the line plotted for this triage system shows that the losses are much larger. This shows that, for this performance measure, the most important feature of the triage performance is that the *FR* rate must be extremely low. Finally, a third line shows what would happen if the triage analysts (together with their summaries) were able to remove 50% of the irrelevant documents, but only falsely discard 5% of the relevant documents. In this case, there is a modest gain for all of the languages. The conclusion is that it is very difficult for a triage analyst to make a significant improvement in *AQWV*.

4.   Tuning the Decision Threshold

Next we look at different ways to use the judgments that result from the triage operation. The first thing we look at is the effect of the threshold on the judgment score. We performed a set of experiments using a Lithuanian corpus of text and audio documents within the MATERIAL program. The CLIR system was run on the Analysis set using the Q1 set of 300 queries. Summaries were generated and

Threshold	Text	Audio
1	64.3	53.9
2	**64.3**	**55.0**
3	72.7	53.0
4	62.2	53.2
5	56.9	51.2
Oracle	73.1	64.6

Table 2: AQWV scores on Lithuanian Analysis set using different acceptance thresholds from 1 to 5. The best results are shown in bold. The last row in the table (Oracle) gives the highest possible values for AQWV if the AMT judges made perfect judgments for this data.

were judged using Amazon Mechanical Turk (AMT). Each judgment was on a scale from 1 to 5, with 1 being clearly irrelevant and 5 being clearly relevant.

Table 2 shows the *AQWV* values for each of the five thresholds, for both Text and Audio. For each threshold, we show the result using the judgments. The result with the highest *AQWV* for each condition is shown in bold.

A threshold of 1 means all documents will be accepted, and therefore gives the *AQWV* obtained by the CLIR system. For both text and audio, we see that there is a modest gain for text and a larger gain for audio data. Using thresholds greater than 2 gives worse results than the original *CLIR* (threshold 1).

For reference, we also show in the last row of Table 2 (labeled 'Oracle') the *AQWV* that we would get if the AMT judges made perfect judgments, i.e., if they judged all relevant documents as relevant and all nonrelevant documents as nonrelevant. Note that these Oracle *AQWV* values are 9-11 points higher than the original *CLIR* values. So, this is the maximum possible gain achievable from perfect summaries and judges. By finding the threshold that maximizes *AQWV* in Table 2, we have narrowed that gap a little. Of course, a different system might have a different optimal threshold. So the optimal threshold for a system must be determined empirically.

We shall see below that the gap can be narrowed further by including the CLIR score in our optimization. As can be seen in Table 2, even with the optimal threshold, the gain in *AQWV* for using the judgments is a small fraction of the upper bound. So the question is whether there is any other way to use the scores to get better results.

5. Optimizing End-to-End (E2E) Performance

In the previous section, we discussed the improvement in *AQWV* that we might get if we replace the relevance score for each document, produced by the CLIR system with the judgment score produced by the Triage analyst and used an acceptance threshold. But the CLIR relevance score also contains very useful information. We maintain that, in order to optimize E2E performance, we should make use of both CLIR and Triage scores in making the final decision. Our proposal is to combine the CLIR relevance and Triage judgment scores (analogous to what we normally do in system combination). A simple weighted linear combination

Interpolation weight w	Text	Audio
0.0 (only AMT score)	64.3	55.0
0.3	**65.6**	57.3
0.7	65.3	**57.9**
1.0 (only CLIR score)	64.3	53.9
Oracle	73.1	64.6

Table 3: Results for combining AMT score with CLIR score (scaled linearly to 1 to 5) as a function of the interpolation weight w. Best results are shown in bold.

of the two scores for each document is given by:

$$Combined_{score} = w \times CLIR_{score} + (1-w) \times Triage_{score}$$

(9)

where $0 \leq w \leq 1$. We then find the value of w that maximizes *AQWV* for a particular system and condition (text or audio).

Before combining the scores, we first scale all the CLIR scores (for text and audio separately) linearly to occupy the same range as the Triage scores (1-5). In this way, this simple combination mechanism above might be applied to CLIR systems with different types of scores. (One could obviously use a more complex nonlinear combination or learn the optimal combination from a small amount of labeled data. But we wanted to make the point by keeping this really simple.)

In Table 3, we show the results of an E2E experiment using the results of the same CLIR/Triage experiment for Lithuanian reported above. We sweep weight w from 0 (only Triage score) to 1 (only CLIR score). For each value of w, we find the threshold on the combined score that gives the highest value of *AQWV*. The first row in the table (weight 0) are the same values shown in Table 2 for threshold 2, and the row with weight 1.0 are the AQWV values using CLIR scores only. As can be seen from this table, it is possible to improve on overall results by combining Triage and CLIR scores. The improvement for text is 1.3 points and 2.9 points for audio over the best *AQWV* values from using the optimal thresholds for AMT scores.

By comparing the bold numbers in Table 3 with the Oracle numbers in Table 2, we see that the gap has narrowed to about 7 points.

In fairness, we should point out that the weight and the threshold were optimized on the same data on which we measure performance. In a proper procedure, we should estimate these 2 parameters on a held out tuning set. However, since we have 300 queries and 1000 returned documents, we do not believe the results would change much. As we can see in Table 2, the performance does not even change very much between weights of 0.3 and 0.7. So we do not believe these results are unrealistic.

6. Discussion

The simple experiments performed here show that, even though it is very difficult to improve on the CLIR result alone, it is possible to get some improvements if we use the scores in an appropriate way. Undoubtedly, there are better ways of combining the judgment and CLIR scores. These methods were just the simplest reasonable methods.

One reason that the maximum benefit for discarding documents is that we use the same value of β for optimizing the initial CLIR threshold and for scoring the final result after the Triage operation. If we had used a lower value of β for the first stage, thereby returning more documents from the CLIR, there would be more relevant documents and there would be a chance for a higher final AQWV score. Of course, this would come at the cost of having to judge more documents in the Triage stage.

7. Conclusion

We have examined the AQWV measure and the effect it has in a CLIR system with a human Triage component. We have shown that the nature of the measure in our system when optimized system results in a relatively small loss due to false alarms. This in turn, makes it difficult to obtain further gains by using human judgments to remove those false alarms. We showed that if human judgments are used, the scores of the judgments are most powerful if they are combined with all other scores in order to derive the most benefit.

8. Acknowledgements

The system used for all of these measurements was the FLAIR System within the MATERIAL program (Zhang et al., 2020). So we thank all of the people involved in building that system.

This work was supported by the Intelligence Advanced Research Projects Activity (IARPA) via Department of Defense US Air Force Research Laboratory contract number FA8650-17-C-9118.

9. Bibliographical References

Alumäe, T., Karakos, D., Hartmann, W., Hsiao, R., Zhang, L., Nguyen, L., Tsakalidis, S., and Schwartz, R. M. (2017). The 2016 BBN georgian telephone speech keyword spotting system. In *2017 IEEE International Conference on Acoustics, Speech and Signal Processing, ICASSP 2017, New Orleans, LA, USA, March 5-9, 2017*, pages 5755–5759. IEEE.

Karakos, D., Schwartz, R. M., Tsakalidis, S., Zhang, L., Ranjan, S., Ng, T., Hsiao, R., Saikumar, G., Bulyko, I., Nguyen, L., Makhoul, J., Grézl, F., Hannemann, M., Karafiát, M., Szöke, I., Veselý, K., Lamel, L., and Le, V. B. (2013). Score normalization and system combination for improved keyword spotting. In *2013 IEEE Workshop on Automatic Speech Recognition and Understanding, Olomouc, Czech Republic, December 8-12, 2013*, pages 210–215. IEEE.

Manning, C. D., Raghavan, P., and Schütze, H. (2008). *Introduction to Information Retrieval*. Cambridge University Press.

Zhang, L., Karakos, D., Hartmann, W., Srivastava, M., Tarlin, L., Akodes, D., Gouda, S. K., Bathool, N., Zhao, L., Jiang, Z., Schwartz, R., and Makhoul, J. (2020). The 2019 bbn cross-lingual information retrieval system. In *Proceedings of LREC Workshop on Cross-Language Search and Summarization of Text and Speech, Marseille, France, 2020*.

Proceedings of the Cross-Language Search and Summarization of Text and Speech Workshop, pages 58–67
Language Resources and Evaluation Conference (LREC 2020), Marseille, 11–16 May 2020
© European Language Resources Association (ELRA), licensed under CC-BY-NC

An Investigative Study of Multi-Modal Cross-Lingual Retrieval

Piyush Arora[*†], **Dimitar Shterionov, Yasufumi Moriya, Abhishek Kaushik,**
Daria Dzendzik, Gareth J. F. Jones
[*]American Express AI Labs, Bangalore, India
ADAPT Centre Dublin City University, Dublin, Ireland
{firstname.lastname1}@aexp.com[*], {firstname.lastname}@adaptcentre.ie

Abstract

We describe work from our investigations of the novel area of multi-modal cross-lingual retrieval (MMCLIR) under low-resource conditions. We study the challenges associated with MMCLIR relating to: (i) data conversion between different modalities, for example speech and text, (ii) overcoming the language barrier between source and target languages; (iii) effectively scoring and ranking documents to suit the retrieval task; and (iv) handling low resource constraints that prohibit development of heavily tuned machine translation (MT) and automatic speech recognition (ASR) systems. We focus on the use case of retrieving text and speech documents in Swahili, using English queries, which was the main focus of the OpenCLIR shared task. Our work is developed within the scope of this task. In this paper we devote special attention to the automatic translation (AT) component which is crucial for the overall quality of the MMCLIR system. We exploit a combination of dictionaries and phrase-based statistical machine translation (SMT) systems to tackle effectively the subtask of query translation. We address each MMCLIR challenge individually, and develop separate components for automatic translation (AT), speech processing (SP) and information retrieval (IR). We find that results with respect to cross-lingual text retrieval are quite good relative to the task of cross-lingual speech retrieval. Overall we find that the task of MMCLIR and specifically cross-lingual speech retrieval is quite complex. Further we highlight open issues related to handling cross-lingual audio and text retrieval for low resource languages that need to be addressed in future research.

Keywords: Multimodal Retrieval, Cross Language Text Retrieval, Cross Language Speech Retrieval, Low resource language

1 Introduction

Cross-lingual information retrieval (CLIR) is an extension of the information retrieval (IR) task where query and documents are in different languages (Oard and Dorr, 1996). The goal of CLIR is to retrieve documents matching a user's query to satisfy their information need. In general, a user would pose a query in their own language (L1), retrieve a document in a foreign language (L2) that is translated into the user's language L1. Machine translation (MT) of some form is thus one of the fundamental components in enabling CLIR (Oard and Dorr, 1996). CLIR has been the focus of much research since its definition in the 1990s. Since this time significant progress have been made in CLIR, and in the associated research areas of automatic speech recognition (ASR) and machine translation (MT). However not much work has been done in the area of multi-modal cross-lingual retrieval (MMCLIR), apart from notable examples such as (Yarmohammadi et al., 2019; Zbib et al., 2019; Boschee et al., 2019), which bring these topics together.

With the increasing interest in information access for diverse multimodal content, there is a need to learn and provide better retrieval tools and technologies to support users, in their desire to satisfy their information needs and quest for new knowledge. The expanding volume and diversity of data made electronically available every day pushes the limits of IR research and development further to facilitate retrieval over different modalities, i.e., multi-modal IR (Chang et al., 2019). This work is a step in this direction to investigate and study the challenges and the performance

of MMCLIR while combining individual component solutions of MT+IR+SP for MMCLIR, and in particular the situation where limited training resources for the technologies are available.

The MMCLIR task rests around four main pillars which need to be addressed adequately both independently and in combination:

1. **Cross-lingualism**: input queries and documents to be retrieved are in different languages;
2. **Document and query modalities**: documents to be retrieved can be in different modalities than the query, but also differ among themselves e.g. text documents and audio recordings;
3. **Information retrieval**: in which the IR mechanism depends on document indexing, query processing, ranking and retrieval,
4. **Low resource constraints**: how to build effective models without having access to the resources typical for MT and speech systems is a major challenge for MMCLIR tasks.

OpenCLIR challenge campaign: This benchmark challenge[1] focused on cross-lingual text and speech retrieval, under a low-resource data setting. In this challenge there was insufficient parallel data available to train state-of-the-art MT and ASR systems. In this task, queries are written (text) keywords in English and the documents are text or audio in Swahili. The work presented in this paper was conducted within the scope of this challenge. We outline the data provided by the OpenCLIR task organizers later (see Section 4) and report our results and findings from the

---

[†]This work was done when the author was a Postdoctoral Researcher at the ADAPT Centre, Dublin City University

[1]https://www.nist.gov/itl/iad/mig/openclir-evaluation

OpenCLIR evaluation.

We investigate a general mechanism for MMCLIR, which can be applied for other such similar low resource languages for which there is insufficient data to train effective MT, ASR and IR systems. Having this use case in mind we present our analysis of the challenges and alternative solutions guided by the aforementioned four pillars.

The main contributions of our work are as follows:

1. We explore not only the strengths and weaknesses of various paradigms for automatic translation: dictionaries, phrase-based statistical machine translation (PB-SMT), but we also combine these into a hybrid system for query translation that optimises the performance of the MMCLIR pipeline.

2. We investigate how different components (MT, ASR and IR) perform in a MMCLIR pipeline, and whether decent scores and performance are obtainable while combining SOTA components for addressing the MMCLIR problem.

3. We assess challenges and provide solutions related to the different pillars of MMCLIR that could serve as baselines for future research on this task.

In this study we pose the following research questions:

1. **RQ1**: Can we exploit alternative automatic translation (AT) approaches for effective query translation in the context of low-resource limitations?

2. **RQ2**: Can we use the most effective state-of-the-art MT, ASR and IR models under the conditions set by our use case to develop a reasonable model for MMCLIR?

This paper is organised as follows. In Section 2 we discuss related work. Section 3 presents our pipeline framework. Our use case and data are discussed in Section 4. We address the main pillars in Section 5, Section 6 and Section 7. Our results and analysis are presented in Section 8. In Section 9 we conclude and present future research directions.

2 Related Work

The strategy for crossing the language barrier between queries and documents in CLIR can be either query translation, document translation or both. Document translation is the preferred method when users need to both search and access documents in their own language (L1) (Croft et al., 1991; Buckley et al., 1997). In query translation, the query is translated into the target language (L2), and then used to retrieve indexed documents in the original language L2 (Oard et al., 2008; Narasimha Raju et al., 2014).

Multiple approaches have been explored to address query translation (sub)task over the years. These can be divided into several categories: dictionary-based, MT-based, corpus-based and ontology-based (Monti et al., 2013). Dictionary-based methods were predominant in early work on query translation (Hull and Grefenstette, 1996; Pirkola et al., 2001; Levow et al., 2005). However, out-of-vocabulary (OOV) issues may easily arise as these dictionaries are limited and require exact matches, thus the whole IR performance may be negatively impacted.

In corpus-based approaches translations of keywords in L1 are extracted from parallel or comparable corpora in L2 based on statistical methods (Picchi and Peters, 1998; Littman et al., 1998). Improvements in MT systems mean that most recent work on CLIR has focused on the use of MT for query translation (Leuski et al., 2003; Madankar et al., 2016). State-of-the-art MT now uses neural approaches (NMT) (Bahdanau et al., 2015; Vaswani et al., 2017). However, it is challenging to train effective NMT systems using limited amounts of parallel data, thus our work focuses on statistical MT approaches.

Recent work on MMCLIR has focused on document translation (Yarmohammadi et al., 2019) using SMT and NMT, learning a shared embeddings space for both queries and documents (Boschee et al., 2019), and learning better word translation probabilities using neural network (Zbib et al., 2019). The authors found that retrieval results using SMT for document translation are relatively better than NMT, possibly due to the limited nature of data (Yarmohammadi et al., 2019). A neural network based approach has also been explored to estimate word translation probabilities for CLIR (Zbib et al., 2019). The authors found that the neural network model estimates better probabilities for word translations than automatic word alignments alone, since using neural network they can encode the character sequences of input source words to generate translations of out-of-vocabulary words.

Following on from our overview, the approach adopted in this paper aims to address our task using a combination of dictionary and statistical MT due to the very limited amounts of bilingual training data available and initial findings that retrieval performance is relatively better when using SMT rather than NMT for CLIR (Yarmohammadi et al., 2019).

3 Approach

For our experiments, we used an MT system to translate the input queries from English to Swahili (described later in Section 5). As the resources available for building translation models were very limited, we focused on translation of input queries rather than attempting to translate the target documents.

We divided our investigation of the MMCLIR task into two phases:

1. **text-based retrieval**: performing retrieval on the Swahili text documents as monolingual retrieval using queries translated from English to Swahili (details on retrieval approach described later in Section 7).

2. **speech-based retrieval**: performing retrieval on the Swahili speech documents using translated queries. In this approach we explored three different alternative approaches for speech-based retrieval: i) generating ASR transcripts, ii) keyword search and iii) phoneme search (all three approaches to speech-based retrieval are described later in Section 6).

For performing document retrieval, we explored data fusion and combination techniques for ranking documents, details are provided later in Section 7.

The system architectures for our text- and speech-based retrieval methods are shown in Figure 1 and Figure 2, respectively. The main components of our system are: i) an MT system (described later in Section 5), ii) an IR system (described later in Section 7), iii) speech processing systems (described later in Section 6)

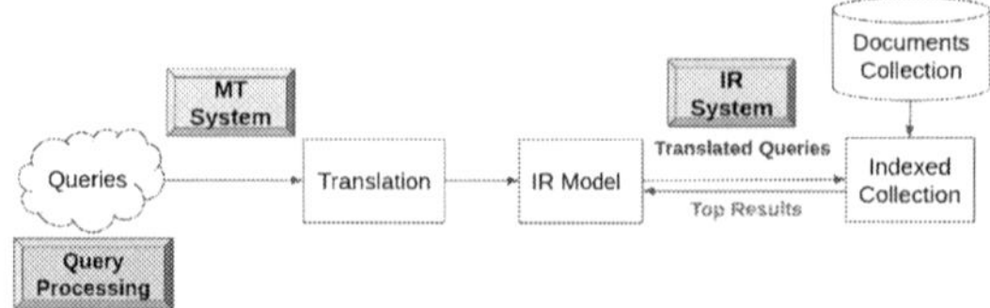

Figure 1: System architecture for text-based retrieval

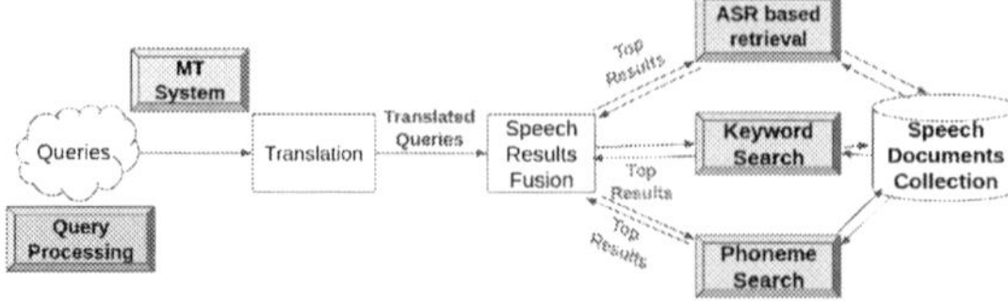

Figure 2: System architecture for speech-based retrieval

Next, we describe the dataset provided for the CLIR task.

4 Dataset & Evaluation mechanism

In this section we describe the dataset used to train MT and ASR systems, and to tune the retrieval system to address the task of text and speech retrieval. We also describe the evaluation mechanism used for this task.

4.1. BUILD corpus

We were provided a BUILD corpus to train the MT and ASR systems by NIST as a part of the OpenCLIR benchmark evaluation. The corpus is described below:

Machine Translation: The data provided by the organisers comprised of $800,000$ words of bitext for MT training. It contained $24,900$ Swahili sentences and their corresponding English translations. In Section 5.1. we provide more details about the external data we used for our translation system.

Speech corpus: We were provided with 50 hours of audio for training the ASR system, the OpenCLIR organizers recommended using 40 and 10 hours of the audio data for training and development purposed respectively.

4.2. Information Retrieval data set

The gold dataset for developing and tuning the IR model was of three types: i) analysis, ii) development, and iii) evaluation. The composition of documents (both speech and text) within all three phases varied as per shown in Table 1.

Phase	No. of text docs	No. of speech docs
Analysis	112	88
Development	101	76
Evaluation	5269	1217

Table 1: Number of documents (docs) for text and speech categories across three phases.

We had a common set of 350 queries for the analysis and development phase and another set of 350 queries for the

evaluation phase. We were provided with relevance judgements for the $ANALYSIS$ corpus to gauge the performance of our models and perform error analysis to develop effective models for retrieving text and speech documents. We were also provided with human translated and transcribed data for the text and speech documents for the analysis set. We had to submit our results to the OpenCLIR evaluation portal to get system scores on the development and evaluation sets. More details on alternative approaches explored in this work and the corresponding performance is provided in Section 8.

4.3. Task evaluation

The evaluation mechanism adopted in this task sought to capture the effectiveness of the system by retrieving more relevant documents (thus minimizing false negatives, i.e. documents which are relevant, but marked as non-relevant by the system) and minimizing the errors made by the system (reducing false positives, i.e. documents which are non-relevant but marked as relevant by the system). A combined measure, shown in Equation 1, is used as an official evaluation measure[2], qv represents score for a query, for a system the qv scores for different queries are averaged and reported as $aqwv$ scores.

$$QV(Q,\theta) = 1 - [P_{Miss}(Q,\theta) + \beta * P_{FA}(Q,\theta)] \quad (1)$$

where θ is an IR threshold to tune the system to maximize QV scores, P_Miss is the false negative probability, P_FA is the false positive probability and β is a penalty factor which was set to 20 for this task.

While seeking the best models and exploring different combinations of MT, Speech and IR components on the $Analysis$ set, we measured the system performance by calculating the number of relevant documents retrieved (Recall), the number of retrieved relevant documents (Precision) and the number of queries for which relevant documents are retrieved.

5 Automatic Translation

Automatic Translation (AT)[3] between English and Swahili is a challenging task due to the lack of parallel data available for training high-quality systems. Furthermore, the specifics of the CLIR task, e.g. queries can be single words or phrases with specific constraints, impose additional constraints on how to approach the AT task.

5.1. Training Data for MT

First, we acquired the parallel data for the OpenCLIR 2019 shared task, i.e. the BUILD corpus. We also acquired and experimented with extra resources aiming to give better translation coverage. We first extended the BUILD data with the Tanzil dataset (http://tanzil.

---

[3]Terms automatic translation and machine translation are used interchangeably, however AT captures dictionary as well as MT systems trained using parallel corpus in this work.

	Lang.	Tokens	ASL.	< 5	< 10
BUILD	EN	$26,788$	33	79	979
$(22,900)$	SW	$44,672$	30	182	$1,469$
+ Tanzil	EN	$39,648$	22	$2,232$	$27,852$
$(159,853)$	SW	$54,715$	17	$5,615$	$45,784$
+ Tanzil	EN	$61,162$	23	$6,702$	$83,562$
+ sing./plur.	SW	$56,557$	17	$16,857$	$137,382$
$(483,459)$					

Table 2: Statistics of the parallel data used for MT. The unique word count is after preprocessing and without the $2,000$ sentences taken aside as the dev and test sets. The total number of parallel sentences is indicated between parenthesis in the first column. ASL is the average sentence length. The number of sentences with length smaller than 5 and 10 tokens is given in the last two columns.

`net/)` (Tiedemann, 2012) which resulted in a total of $163,153$ parallel sentences. Due to the small amount of data, we opted for phrase-based statistical MT (PB-SMT) (Zens et al., 2002; Koehn et al., 2003) which handles translations at a phrase level, and typically requires much less data than building an NMT system. Details on our MT systems are presented in Section 5.2.

After conducting initial CLIR experiments with the aforementioned system we noticed that many plural/singular words are not translated, while their singular/plural forms are. Since this will impede overall IR performance more than if a translation is not correct with respect to only the number, we decided to implement a mechanism to deal with nouns in both forms (plurals or singulars). We extended the training data (BUILD + Tanzil) with additional singular and plural versions, where in each sentence all nouns had been converted to their singular and plural forms leading to a triple increase of the translation data. In order to balance the data and not put extra emphasis on part of the data (the part that contains nouns), we made three copies of all sentence pairs, even if they do not contain nouns.

From the original (BUILD) data we randomly extracted $1,000$ sentence pairs as a development set and another $1,000$ as a test set, (leaving $22,900$ sentences in the training set). All data were tokenised and lowercased.

5.2. Core algorithmic approach

Once we had analysed the available data we decided to handle the problem of translation between English and Swahili through word- and phrase-based approaches, i.e. a dictionary and PB-SMT systems.

Dictionary: We used the resources provided by `http://swahili.vickio.net/dictionary/`, containing 25,000 words collected via the Kamusi Project (`https://kamusi.org/`). We used dictionaries of Swahili words with English translation which were obtained from `1000 Most Common Words` platform (Swahili[4]), `101languages` (SWAHILI 101[5]), and The

`Swahili-English Dictionary`[6] which is based on Swahili-Kiswahili to English Translation Program by Morris Fried. [7]

We combined these dictionaries and formed a single unified dictionary providing a list of possible Swahili words for the corresponding English query words. Few examples from this combined dictionary where an English word is mapped to multiple possible Swahili words are shown in Table 3.

English word	Swahili words mapped in the dictionary
road	barabara, ndia, njia
congress	bunge, kongamano
refugees	mhamiaji, mkimbizi, mtoro

Table 3: Examples from the combined English-Swahili dictionary.

PB-SMT: Using the data described in Section 5.1. we trained three PB-SMT systems: one for each data set listed in Table 2. Our PB-SMT systems were trained using the MOSES toolkit (Koehn et al., 2007) with default settings and a 5-gram language model. Each system was further tuned with MERT (Och and Ney, 2003) until convergence or for a maximum of 25 iterations. To assess the performance of our MT systems, we used the BLEU evaluation metric (Papineni et al., 2002). Our BLEU scores on the test set are presented in Table 4.

System name	MT type	Training data	BLEU ↑
PB-SMT-B	PB-SMT	BUILD	44.40
PB-SMT-BT	PB-SMT	+Tanzil	41.73
PB-SMT-BTP	PB-SMT	+Tanzil +sing-plur	41.76

Table 4: BLEU scores for our EN→SW PB-SMT systems (higher blue value is the better).

A note on BLEU: The BLEU scores shown in Table 4 indicate that the PB-SMT-B system trained only on the BUILD corpus, performs better than the other PB-SMT systems trained with more data. The main reason is the domain-specific test set that we used – this test set is very similar to the BUILD data – which leads to the higher BLEU scores for systems trained on less data. Furthermore, due to the similarity between the data in the BUILD corpus and the documents to be retrieved, we expect that using MT systems with higher BLEU scores will lead to higher IR performance. However, we are more interested in the overall impact that these systems can have on performance when they are used in combination.

That is, we assess the quality of the alternative translation systems by measuring retrieval performance on the Analysis set (IR results using different translation systems are described later in Section 8). Our retrieval pipeline uses all three MT systems as shown in Table 4 for query translation (described later in Section 7).

---

[4] `http://1000mostcommonwords.com/1000-most-common-swahili-words/`

[5] `https://www.101languages.net/swahili/swahili-word-list/`

[6] `https://www.mimuw.edu.pl/~jsbien/BW/Swa-Eng-xFried/Swa-eng.txt`

[7] `www.dict.org/links.html`

The original query text is passed to each of the MT engines and a translation is generated. For broader coverage of the possible translation we consider the top 3 hypotheses returned by a MT system, under the hypothesis that this can improve IR effectiveness.

6   Speech Processing

Searching for a textual query in speech documents is often performed on speech transcripts of the documents created using an ASR system. In low-resource scenarios, it is difficult to build a high quality ASR system for the target language due to the shortage of labelled speech corpora. To alleviate the quality of our ASR system, we combined output of a keyword spotting system and a phoneme search system with ASR output.

6.1.   Core algorithmic approach

The following three subsections overview conventional ASR, a keyword spotting system and a phoneme search algorithm.

6.1.1.   ASR

The goal of ASR is to transcribe an audio file into speech transcripts. A conventional ASR system consists of an acoustic model, a language model and a pronunciation lexicon. While the acoustic model and language model are often developed with a machine learning approach, the pronunciation lexicon is a list of hand-crafted mapping between words and pronunciations. An acoustic model can be trained on transcribed speech data, and typically consists of a deep neural network (DNN) incorporated into an hidden Markov model (HMM) to compute posterior probabilities of phones (Hinton et al., 2012). The language model is trained on raw text of the target language, and it enforces grammatical constraints on output of an ASR system. For the CLIR task, approximately 50 hours of transcribed speech and corresponding text and a Swahili pronunciation lexicon were provided for the OpenCLIR task (see Section 6.2.). When an ASR system decodes input audio into word strings, it often employs a finite state transducer to represent phone posterior probabilities and word probabilities from which n pre-defined paths of output strings can be recovered (Mohri et al., 2002).

6.1.2.   Keyword search

It is difficult to train a high quality acoustic model and a language model when only small amounts of audio and text data are available. An alternative to ASR for searching spoken documents is a keyword search system. A keyword search system takes as input a query word and a speech document and decides whether the query word is uttered in the document. One of the approaches to keyword search is transforming finite state transducers to a single generalized factor transducer, where each word token of the transducers is stored with its associated scores (Trmal et al., 2017). Given a factor transducer of a speech document and a query word, the keyword search system returns a binary decision whether the query word is in the document.

6.1.3.   Phoneme search

A phoneme search is based only on a sequence of intermediate phoneme representations and a pronunciation lexicon. Given a pronunciation of a query word found in a pronunciation lexicon and a sequence of phonemes corresponding to a speech document, the system searches for an exact match of the phoneme sequence of the query word with a phoneme level transcription of the document. While this approach is likely to induce more false alarms particularly for short query words, by combining this system with ASR and keyword search, it can enrich the content of the search index.

6.2.   Resources and Tools used

We used the Kaldi speech recognition toolkit to build an ASR system (Povey et al., 2011). The acoustic model consists of 6 linear layers with size 1,024 and one output layer to 1,552 context-dependent phones. The input is standard 13 dimensional MFCC speech vectors. The model has a time-delayed architecture (Peddinti et al., 2015). A language model was built using the SRI LM toolkit (Stolcke, 2002). The language model is a 3-gram built using Kneser-Ney interpolation (Chen and Goodman, 1995). For generation of pronunciations of out-of-vocabulary (OOV) words, a squiter G2P model was trained using the provided Swahili pronunciation lexicon.

A Keyword search system was also built using the Kaldi toolkit (Trmal et al., 2017). The toolkit converts decoding lattices generated using our ASR system to a generalized factor transducer of word tokens. The system then decides whether a query word exists in the given collection of speech documents.

Phone strings of utterances for phoneme search were generated using a decoded lattice of ASR. Based on translated queries of Swahili and given strings, queries are matched with entries in the pronunciation lexicon. When corresponding entries are missing, the G2P model was applied to the queries to obtain pronunciation of the queries. Then, exact matching of the pronunciation of queries with phoneme strings was performed based on a regular expression.

6.3.   Data processing

Since the Kaldi speech recognition toolkit randomly selects a portion of speech data for a validation set on the fly, all of the provided speech data belonging to the "BUILD" partition was used for training of an acoustic model. Speech data was segmented into shorter speech utterances based on time-stamps of transcripts of phone conversation, because excessively long speech data leads to inefficient decoding. The "Evaluation" set was, however, not provided with time-stamped transcripts. Therefore, we decoded the "Eval" set once without segmenting it, and then created shorter utterances of the "Eval" set based on silence points in speech, in order to keep the maximum duration of speech utterance to 30 seconds. For training our language model, we used the provided speech transcripts of the training set and the external Tanzil dataset mentioned in Section 5.1.

	Example-1	Example-2
English query word	kick	messenger
PB-SMT-B	kiki	messenger
PB-SMT-BT	kiki	mtume
PB-SMT-BTP	kiki	mtume
PB-SMT-B top K words	piga; kiki	messenger
PB-SMT-BT top K words	kiki; kumpiga piga	mtume;mjumbe; mitume
PB-SMT-BTP top K words	kiki; kumpiga piga	mtume;mjumbe; mitume
Dictionary mapping	teke; kiki	mjumbe;mshenga; mtume;rasuli; tarishi;tume

Table 5: Examples of input query translation for an MT system. The translated hypotheses are sorted in decreasing order of translation scores.

7 Information Retrieval

In this section we describe the different components of our IR system, and present the tools and resources that are used for the development of the IR components.

7.1. Resources used and Data pre-processing

We used whoosh version 2.7.4, a python based library of classes and functions for performing IR operations such as indexing of documents and searching over the indexed collection.

Stopwords: We obtained top 10 words based on the term frequency in the document collection. We experimented with indexing and searching with and without stopwords, we found that retrieval results using stopwords are relatively better for our CLIR task. Our Swahili stopword list comprised of the following 10 words: "ya", "wa", "na", "kwa", "katika", "la", "za", "ni", "le", "cha".

7.2. Document indexing

For text-based retrieval and speech-based retrieval using ASR transcripts, we indexed the documents using the whoosh indexer. We removed stopwords and all non-alphanumeric keys from the data before indexing the raw documents. We maintained two separate indexes for text- and speech-based retrieval. We used these indexed collections to retrieve documents matching a given input query. After query processing, the input queries are translated using the MT component described in Section 5. Thus for each of the input queries we have multiple translated candidates as shown in Table 5.

7.3. Document retrieval and ranking

To retrieve and rank documents effectively for a given query over the indexed collection we use the BM25 model (Robertson et al., 1995). BM25 is a probabilistic model that assigns a probability score to each document indicating its relevance to a given query. The investigations of document retrieval and ranking focused on two main aspects:

1. **Query translation selection (QTS)**: As shown above in Table 5, we have multiple possible translation hypothesis for a given query. We explored alternative methods to select and retrieve results corresponding to different translation hypotheses.

2. **Optimum threshold detection (OTD)**: The focus of the task is to maximize the number of relevant documents and minimize the number of non-relevant documents retrieved by the developed model. Thus we focus on selecting different cut-off rank to prune the retrieved ranked list to maximise measured retrieval effectiveness.

To find effective QTS and OTD techniques to boost retrieval performance we experimented with the *Analysis* set. As described earlier in Table 1, we have gold relevance judgments (*qrels*) for the Analysis set, where for a set of queries we have corresponding relevant text and speech documents which can be used to develop and tune the text and speech retrieval models for optimal performance.

As shown in Table 6, the distribution of relevant documents across queries varies considerably for both the textual and speech collections. In the *analysis* set about 43% of the queries have no relevant documents. About 2% of the queries have 10 or more relevant documents, with the maximum number of relevant documents being 18. The *analysis* set is just 112 and 88 documents for text- and speech data respectively which is much less than the *evaluation* set which has 5269 and 1217 documents, for text- and speech data respectively. Varying the size of the collections poses challenges for effective tuning of the system, such as determining the best cut-off rank for pruning the retrieved ranked list. We explored different cut-off ranks $[10, 15, 20]$ for the analysis set and $[50, 100, 200]$ for the evaluation set in our experiments.

	Total Queries	Queries with RR	No. of rel docs
Complete dataset	350	198	491
Text documents only	198	166	339
Speech documents only	198	99	152

Table 6: Distribution of relevance judgements for the analysis set. RR indicates relevant results, rel docs indicates the number of relevant documents

8 Results and Analysis

In this section we present our results on the analysis set for text- and speech-based retrieval before moving on to present our results on the evaluation set.[8]

8.1. Results on the Analysis set

Table 7 shows our results using different translation methods for the input queries for both text- and speech-based retrieval using the ASR approach. Due to the absence of other comparative models, we present retrieval results using queries translated using the Google translation engine[9] as a comparison for the behaviour of different MT systems explored in our work. We found that all alternative translation

---

[8]Due to space limitations we avoid results on development set as the composition of the development set is similar to analysis set, and instead present results with respect to the analysis and evaluation sets, which have quite different document collection sizes.

[9]https://translate.google.com/

Model	System	Text Retrieval				Speech Retrieval using only ASR			
		Recall ↑	Precision↑	AQWV↑	Rel Q ↑	Recall ↑	Precision↑	AQWV↑	Rel Q ↑
Google Translation		0.377	0.367	0.242	76	0.118	0.130	0.045	14
PB-SMT-B	MT-1	0.307	0.380	**0.202**	59	0.066	0.108	**0.015**	7
PB-SMT-BTP	MT-2	0.301	0.301	0.155	66	0.072	0.094	0.008	11
PB-SMT-BT	MT-3	0.295	0.376	0.193	59	0.066	0.104	0.013	9
PB-SMT-B top 3 hypotheses	MT-4	0.339	0.311	0.182	69	0.125	0.074	-0.020	14
PB-SMT-BTP top 3 hypotheses	MT-5	0.345	0.185	0.028	78	0.131	0.048	-0.112	18
PB-SMT-BT top 3 hypotheses	MT-6	0.319	0.268	0.137	67	0.092	0.051	-0.068	13
Dictionary	MT-7	0.407	0.191	0.047	76	0.105	0.050	-0.082	13

Table 7: Results on the Analysis set for text- and speech-based retrieval using only the ASR approach, where Rel Q indicates the number of relevant queries found by the system having atleast one relevant document, best scores are in bold face

models appear to find complementary relevant documents for different types of query as shown in Table 7.

Next, we explored combination approaches where we exploited the query translation results from different translation models. We explored an interpolation mechanism where we used a combination of MT systems (list of MT systems) for query translation, we perform query translation using the first MT system, and if we find no results using this first translation system for an input query, we perform query translation using the second translation system from the list of MT systems. For example for a translation system using a combination of $MT - 1$, $MT - 2$ and $MT - 3$, first we perform search using the query translated through system $MT - 1$, and if we retrieve zero results, we perform search using the query translated through system $MT - 2$, and repeat until documents are retrieved or all MT systems have been tried. We find in our investigation that combining MT systems in this linear interpolated manner leads to less false positives (non-relevant results identified as relevant). The results of different interpolation approaches investigated in our work for both text- and speech-based retrieval are presented in Table 8. The best scoring MT systems are selected for carrying experiments on the evaluation set.

Table 7 and Table 8 show the best results for the analysis set which correspond to a cut-off rank of 20, where for each query we just retrieve and return the top 20 results. Table 9 shows the variations in the results for text- and speech-based retrieval while varying the number of top k documents retrieved using the MT-1 translation system. Table 10 presents results of the alternative speech retrieval approaches explored in our work. In the combined model for speech retrieval we combine the output of alternative retrieval approaches (ASR, Keyword search, and Phoneme search) to formulate a single ranked list for a given query. For Keyword and Phoneme search we used queries translated using PB-SMT-B (MT-1) system. There is a considerable difference in the speech retrieval results on the human transcribed data and the ASR results as shown in Table 10, indicating the need to improve the quality of ASR outputs.

8.2. Results on the Evaluation set

The main variations that we explore for the evaluation set correspond to: i) exploring the top MT systems and their

combinations, and ii) varying the document cut-off ranks to [50, 100, 200] for pruning the relevant results. There is a considerable difference in the cut-off rank for the analysis and evaluation sets, since the size of evaluation document collection is relatively bigger than the analysis document collection. Table 11 presents the results of our models on the evaluation set for text- and speech-based retrieval.

Main Findings and Challenges: In our work the best retrieval scores are attained by MT model combining the output of Dictionary + PBMT. We find it is better to combine the output of multiple MT systems rather than to rely on one best MT system for cross-lingual retrieval. The speech retrieval scores are relatively poor, reflecting that cross-lingual speech retrieval is quite a complex problem. Based on our analysis we can conclude that we need better methods and models for leveraging information from the different MT systems and the speech processing models to boost retrieval performance.

We investigated alternative methods for text- and speech-based retrieval. These are not the best results as we focus on the combination of different modules in a greedy manner rather than exploring the optimal best combination of the whole pipeline. We were interested in finding the individual best MT, Speech and IR systems and combining these to address the task of MMCLIR. Using the limited relevance judgments that were available for the analysis set, and the limited feedback provided on the evaluation set, we combined and investigated alternative approaches and explored different cut-off ranks for retrieving documents. We anticipate that given a larger relevance dataset ($qrels\ judgement$), we would be able to combine these different components more effectively to boost the retrieval performance. We learnt that unlike traditional MT modules and Speech modules, a combination of diverse MT systems, which capture diverse information, performs better overall for the MMLCIR task as indicated in Table 8.

9 Conclusion and Future work

In this work we investigated a MMCLIR task focusing on English-Swahili search carried out within the OpenCLIR challenge. We examine solutions to several challenges for MMCLIR in the context of low-resource availability. We investigated two research questions and examined alternative AT approaches for effective query translation. We build

MT Systems	Text Retrieval				Speech Retrieval using only ASR			
	Recall ↑	Precision↑	AQWV↑	Rel Q ↑	Recall ↑	Precision↑	AQWV↑	Rel Q ↑
MT-1+MT-2	0.354	0.397	0.242	73	0.092	0.122	0.030	10
MT-1+MT-2+MT-3	0.363	0.386	0.242	74	0.112	0.130	**0.042**	13
MT-1+MT-2+MT-4	0.372	0.341	0.222	79	0.131	0.079	-0.011	15
MT-1+MT-2+MT-7	0.466	0.280	0.216	99	0.118	0.061	-0.050	14
MT-1+MT-2+MT-3+MT-4	0.378	0.332	0.219	79	0.145	0.083	-0.004	17
MT-1+MT-2+MT-3+MT-7	0.460	0.273	0.205	97	0.125	0.063	-0.048	15
MT-1+MT-2+MT-4+MT-7	0.475	0.308	**0.253**	102	0.151	0.067	-0.043	18
MT-1+MT-2+MT-3+MT-4-MT-7	0.469	0.301	0.242	100	0.158	0.069	-0.041	19

Table 8: Interpolation model exploration, where Rel Q indicates the number of relevant queries found by the system having atleast one relevant document, best scores are in bold face, results on the Analysis set

Rank K	Text Retrieval			Speech Retrieval using only ASR		
	Recall↑	Precision ↑	AQWV scores↑	Recall↑	Precision ↑	AQWV scores↑
10	0.3038	0.4345	0.2214	0.0590	0.1058	0.0128
15	0.3067	0.3950	0.2090	0.0660	0.1075	0.0150
20	0.3067	0.3795	0.2022	0.0660	0.1075	0.0150
All results	0.3067	0.3795	0.2022	0.0660	0.1075	0.0150

Table 9: Optimum threshold selection, using MT-1 translation system, results on the Analysis set

Speech System	Recall↑	Rel Q↑	Precision ↑	AQWV scores↑
Using Human Transcriptions	0.2500	30	0.3064	0.1974
Using ASR (Single best MT)	0.0660	7	0.1075	0.0150
Phoneme Search	0.1052	12	0.0443	-0.1056
Keyword Spotting	0.0789	9	0.1237	**0.0269**
Combined	0.0197	22	0.0667	-0.0593

Table 10: Speech results on the Analysis set, where Rel Q indicates the number of relevant queries found by the system, best scores are in bold face

System Settings	Text Retrieval			System Settings	Speech Retrieval		
	P_MISS_REL ↓	P_FA ↓	AQWV↑		P_MISS_REL ↓	P_FA ↓	AQWV↑
Google, k=50	0.6933	0.0013	0.2804	**ASR Google**, k=50	0.8691	0.0047	**0.0362**
Google, k=100	0.6710	0.0020	0.2896	ASR Google, k=100	0.8603	0.0058	0.0240
Google, k=200	0.6590	0.0027	0.2864	ASR Google, k=200	0.8584	0.0066	0.0103
Sys-1, k=50	0.8005	0.0007	0.1853	ASR Sys-1, k=50	0.9213	0.0027	0.0255
Sys-1, k=100	0.7836	0.0011	0.1947	ASR Sys-1, k=100	0.9174	0.0034	0.0137
Sys-1, k=200	0.7756	0.0016	0.1934	ASR Sys-1, k=200	0.9162	0.0038	0.0074
Sys-2, k=50	0.6730	0.0011	0.3047	ASR Sys-2, k=50	0.9044	0.0037	0.0214
Sys-2, k=100	0.6535	0.0016	**0.3140**	ASR Sys-2, k=100	0.8980	0.0048	0.0058
Sys-2, k=200	0.6444	0.0022	0.3116	ASR Sys-2, k=200	0.8967	0.0054	-0.0050
–	–	–	–	Phoneme Search	0.9511	0.0011	0.0260
–	–	–	–	Keyword Search	0.9879	0.0043	-0.0736
–	–	–	–	Combined	0.9213	0.0027	0.0255

Table 11: Results on the evaluation set, Google and ASR Google indicates using Google translation, Sys-1 and ASR Sys-1 corresponds to the single best MT-1 translation system, Sys-2 corresponds to the MT combination system representing: <MT-1, MT-2, MT-4, MT-7> system, and ASR Sys-2 corresponds to the MT combination system representing: <MT-1, MT-2, MT-3> systems

an end to end system for MMCLIR using state-of-the-art MT, ASR and IR models. The retrieval scores are quite low, specifically for cross-lingual speech-based retrieval, indicating that there is likely to be quite some scope for improvement. There is a need to explore diverse mechanisms such as effective combination of multiple outputs to address the complex problem of MMCLIR involving multiple modalities and multiple languages.

We anticipate that work on MMCLIR will open new avenues and increase the scope of future research and promote interesting new research collaborations and pathways as the amount of multi-modal content is expected to rise very significantly as we consume and interact with more applications and content (Chang et al., 2019). In the future we would like to be able to explore new language pairs, and already plan to work on building better MT and Speech models to boost retrieval effectiveness.

Acknowledgement

This research is supported by Science Foundation Ireland (SFI) as a part of the ADAPT Centre at Dublin City University (Grant No: 12/CE/I2267).

10   Bibliographical References

Bahdanau, D., Cho, K., and Bengio, Y. (2015). Neural Machine Translation by Jointly Learning to Align and Translate. In *Proceedings of International Conference on Learning Representations (ICLR2015)*, San Diego, USA, May.

Boschee, E., Barry, J., Billa, J., Freedman, M., Gowda, T., Lignos, C., Palen-Michel, C., Pust, M., Khonglah, B. K., Madikeri, S., et al. (2019). Saral: A low-resource cross-lingual domain-focused information retrieval system for effective rapid document triage. In *Proceedings of the 57th Annual Meeting of the Association for Computational Linguistics: System Demonstrations*, pages 19–24.

Buckley, C., Mitra, M., Walz, J. A., and Cardie, C. (1997). Using clustering and superconcepts within SMART: TREC 6. In *Proceedings of The Sixth Text REtrieval Conference, TREC 1997, Gaithersburg, Maryland, USA, November 19-21, 1997*, pages 107–124.

Chang, S.-F., Hauptmann, A., and Morency, L.-P. (2019). Key challenges for multimedia research in the next ten years.

Chen, S. F. and Goodman, J. (1995). An empirical study of smoothing techniques for language modeling. *Computer Speech and Language*, pages 310–318.

Croft, W. B., Turtle, H. R., and Lewis, D. D. (1991). The use of phrases and structured queries in information retrieval. In *Proceedings of the 14th Annual International ACM SIGIR Conference on Research and Development in Information Retrieval. Chicago, Illinois, USA, October 13-16, 1991 (Special Issue of the SIGIR Forum)*, pages 32–45.

Hinton, G., Deng, L., Yu, D., Dahl, G. E., Mohamed, A., Jaitly, N., Senior, A., Vanhoucke, V., Nguyen, P., Sainath, T. N., and Kingsbury, B. (2012). Deep neural networks for acoustic modeling in speech recognition: The shared views of four research groups. *IEEE Signal Processing Magazine*, 29(6):82–97.

Hull, D. A. and Grefenstette, G. (1996). Querying across languages: A dictionary-based approach to multilingual information retrieval. In *Proceedings of the 19th Annual International ACM SIGIR Conference on Research and Development in Information Retrieval*, SIGIR '96, pages 49–57, New York, NY, USA. ACM.

Koehn, P., Och, F. J., and Marcu, D. (2003). Statistical Phrase-based Translation. In *Proceedings of the 2003 Conference of the North American Chapter of the Association for Computational Linguistics on Human Language Technology-Volume 1*, pages 48–54, Edmonton, Cannada.

Koehn, P., Hoang, H., Birch, A., Callison-Burch, C., Federico, M., Bertoldi, N., Cowan, B., Shen, W., Moran, C., Zens, R., Dyer, C., Bojar, O., Constantin, A., and Herbst, E. (2007). Moses: Open-Source Toolkit for Statistical Machine Translation. In *Proceedings of the 45th annual meeting of the ACL on interactive poster and demonstration sessions (ACL2007)*, pages 177–180, Prague, Czech Republic.

Leuski, A., Lin, C., Zhou, L., Germann, U., Och, F. J., and Hovy, E. H. (2003). Cross-lingual c*st*rd: English access to hindi information. *ACM Trans. Asian Lang. Inf. Process.*, 2(3):245–269.

Levow, G.-A., Oard, D. W., and Resnik, P. (2005). Dictionary-based techniques for cross-language information retrieval. *Inf. Process. Manage.*, 41(3):523–547, May.

Littman, M. L., Dumais, S. T., and Landauer, T. K., (1998). *Automatic Cross-Language Information Retrieval Using Latent Semantic Indexing*, pages 51–62. Springer US, Boston, MA.

Madankar, M., Chandak, M., and Chavhan, N. (2016). Information retrieval system and machine translation: A review. *Procedia Computer Science*, 78:845 – 850. 1st International Conference on Information Security Privacy 2015.

Mohri, M., Pereira, F., and Riley, M. (2002). Weighted finite-state transducers in speech recognition. *Computer Speech & Language*, 16(1):69–88.

Monti, J., Monteleone, M., di Buono, M. P., and Marano, F. (2013). Cross-lingual information retrieval and semantic interoperability for cultural heritage repositories. In *Proceedings of the International Conference Recent Advances in Natural Language Processing RANLP 2013*, pages 483–490, Hissar, Bulgaria, September. INCOMA Ltd. Shoumen, BULGARIA.

Narasimha Raju, B. N. V., Bhadri Raju, M. S. V. S., and Satyanarayana, K. V. V. (2014). Translation approaches in cross language information retrieval. In *International Conference on Computing and Communication Technologies*, pages 1–4, Dec.

Oard, D. W. and Dorr, B. J. (1996). A survey of multilingual text retrieval. College Park, MD, USA. University of Maryland at College Park.

Oard, D. W., He, D., and Wang, J. (2008). User-assisted query translation for interactive cross-language information retrieval. *Inf. Process. Manage.*, 44(1):181–211.

Och, F. J. and Ney, H. (2003). A Systematic Comparison of Various Statistical Alignment Models. In *Computational Linguistics, Volume 29:1*, pages 19–51. MIT Press, Cambridge, Massachusetts, USA.

Papineni, K., Roukos, S., Ward, T., and Zhu, W.-J. (2002). BLEU: a Method for Automatic Evaluation of Machine Translation. In *Proceedings of the 40th Annual Meeting on Association for Computational Linguistics (ACL)*, pages 311–318, Philadephia, PA, USA, July.

Peddinti, V., Povey, D., and Khudanpur, S. (2015). A time delay neural network architecture for efficient modeling of long temporal contexts. In *Interspeech*, pages 2–6.

Picchi, E. and Peters, C., (1998). *Cross-Language Information Retrieval: A System for Comparable Corpus Querying*, pages 81–92. Springer US, Boston, MA.

Pirkola, A., Hedlund, T., Keskustalo, H., and Järvelin, K. (2001). Dictionary-based cross-language information retrieval: Problems, methods, and research findings. *Information Retrieval*, 4(3):209–230, Sep.

Povey, D., Ghoshal, A., Boulianne, G., Burget, L., Glembek, O., Goel, N., Hannemann, M., Motlicek, P., Qian, Y., Schwarz, P., Silovsky, J., Stemmer, G., and Vesely, K. (2011). The Kaldi speech recognition toolkit. In *Pro-*

ceedings of IEEE Workshop on Automatic Speech Recognition and Understanding (ASRU), pages 1–4.

Robertson, S., Walker, S., Jones, S., Hancock-Beaulieu, M., and Gatford, M. (1995). Okapi at trec-3. *NIST special publication*, (500225):109–123.

Stolcke, A. (2002). SRILM-an extensible language modeling toolkit. In *International Conference on Spoken Language Processing (ICSLP)*.

Tiedemann, J. (2012). Parallel data, tools and interfaces in OPUS. In *Proceedings of the Eighth International Conference on Language Resources and Evaluation, LREC 2012, Istanbul, Turkey, May 23-25, 2012*, pages 2214–2218.

Trmal, J., Wiesner, M., Peddinti, V., Zhang, X., Ghahremani, P., Wang, Y., Manohar, V., Xu, H., Povey, D., and Khudanpur, S. (2017). The kaldi openkws system: Improving low resource keyword search. In *Proc. Interspeech 2017*, pages 3597–3601.

Vaswani, A., Shazeer, N., Parmar, N., Uszkoreit, J., Jones, L., Gomez, A. N., Kaiser, L., and Polosukhin, I. (2017). Attention is all you need. In *Advances in Neural Information Processing Systems 30: Annual Conference on Neural Information Processing Systems 2017, 4-9 December 2017, Long Beach, CA, USA*, pages 5998–6008.

Yarmohammadi, M., Ma, X., Hisamoto, S., Rahman, M., Wang, Y., Xu, H., Povey, D., Koehn, P., and Duh, K. (2019). Robust document representations for cross-lingual information retrieval in low-resource settings. In *Proceedings of Machine Translation Summit XVII Volume 1: Research Track, MTSummit 2019, Dublin, Ireland, August 19-23, 2019*, pages 12–20.

Zbib, R., Zhao, L., Karakos, D., Hartmann, W., DeYoung, J., Huang, Z., Jiang, Z., Rivkin, N., Zhang, L., Schwartz, R., et al. (2019). Neural-network lexical translation for cross-lingual ir from text and speech. In *Proceedings of the 42nd International ACM SIGIR Conference on Research and Development in Information Retrieval*, pages 645–654.

Zens, R., Och, F. J., and Ney, H. (2002). Phrase-based statistical machine translation. In *KI 2002: Advances in Artificial Intelligence, 25th Annual German Conference on AI, KI 2002, Aachen, Germany, September 16-20, 2002, Proceedings*, pages 18–32.

Proceedings of the Cross-Language Search and Summarization of Text and Speech Workshop, pages 68–73
Language Resources and Evaluation Conference (LREC 2020), Marseille, 11–16 May 2020
© European Language Resources Association (ELRA), licensed under CC-BY-NC

Subtitles to Segmentation: Improving Low-Resource Speech-to-Text Translation Pipelines

**David Wan[1], Zhengping Jiang[1], Chris Kedzie[1], Elsbeth Turcan[1],
Peter Bell[2] and Kathleen McKeown[1]**
[1]Columbia University, [2]University of Edinburgh
{dw2735, zj2265}@columbia.edu, {kedzie,eturcan,kathy}@cs.columbia.edu, peter.bell@ed.ac.uk

Abstract

In this work, we focus on improving ASR output segmentation in the context of low-resource language speech-to-text translation. ASR output segmentation is crucial, as ASR systems segment the input audio using purely acoustic information and are not guaranteed to output sentence-like segments. Since most MT systems expect sentences as input, feeding in longer unsegmented passages can lead to sub-optimal performance. We explore the feasibility of using datasets of subtitles from TV shows and movies to train better ASR segmentation models. We further incorporate part-of-speech (POS) tag and dependency label information (derived from the unsegmented ASR outputs) into our segmentation model. We show that this noisy syntactic information can improve model accuracy. We evaluate our models intrinsically on segmentation quality and extrinsically on downstream MT performance, as well as downstream tasks including cross-lingual information retrieval (CLIR) tasks and human relevance assessments. Our model shows improved performance on downstream tasks for Lithuanian and Bulgarian.

Keywords: Speech Segmentation, Lithuanian, Bulgarian, Low-Resource Languages

1. Introduction

A typical pipeline for speech-to-text translation (STTT) uses a cascade of automatic speech recognition (ASR), ASR output segmentation, and machine translation (MT) components (Cho et al., 2017). ASR output segmentation is crucial, as ASR systems segment the input audio using purely acoustic information and are not guaranteed to output sentence-like segments (i.e., one utterance may be split if the speaker pauses in the middle, or utterances may be combined if the speaker does not pause). Since most MT systems expect sentences as input, feeding in longer unsegmented passages can lead to sub-optimal performance (Koehn and Knowles, 2017).

When the source language is a low-resource language, suitable training data may be very limited for ASR and MT, and even nonexistent for segmentation. Since typical low-resource language ASR audio datasets crawled from the web do not have hand-annotated segments we propose deriving proxy segmentation datasets from TV show and movie subtitles. Subtitles typically contain boundary information like sentence-final punctuation and speaker turn information, even if they are not exact transcriptions.

We further incorporate part-of-speech (POS) tag and dependency label information (derived from the unsegmented ASR outputs) into our segmentation model. This noisy syntactic information can improve model accuracy.

We evaluate our models intrinsically on segmentation quality and extrinsically on downstream MT performance. Since the quality of the underlying MT of low-resource languages is relatively weak, we also extrinsically evaluate our improved STTT pipeline on document and passage-level cross-lingual information retrieval (CLIR) tasks. We report results for two translation settings: Bulgarian (BG) to English and Lithuanian (LT) to English.

This paper makes the following contributions: (i) We propose the use of subtitles as a proxy dataset for ASR segmentation. (ii) We develop a simple neural tagging model using noisy syntactic features on this dataset. (iii) We show downstream performance increases on several extrinsic tasks: MT and document and passage-level CLIR tasks.

2. Related Work

Segmentation in STTT has been studied quite extensively in high resource settings. Earlier models use kernel-based SVM models to predict sentence boundaries from ngram and part-of-speech features derived from a fixed window size (Sridhar et al., 2013).

Recent segmentation models use neural architecture, such as LSTM (Sperber et al., 2018) and Transformer models (Pham et al., 2019). These models benefit from large training data available for the high-resource languages. For example, the STTT task for English audio to German include TED corpus, which contains about 340 hours of well transcribed data. To our knowledge, these data do not exist for the languages we are interested in. In addition, these models predict full punctuation marks as well as casing for words (binary classification of casing). However, since our translation models are trained on unpunctuated texts, we restrict the classification task to predicting full stop boundaries only.

Although recent works have looked at end-to-end speech-to-text translation, in a high-resource setting, these models (Vila et al., 2018) achieved at most a 0.5 BLEU score improvement over a weak cascaded model. In general, the available data for end-to-end neural models is insufficient or non-existent in all but the most specific circumstances; for any pair of languages there will inevitably be far less translated speech data available than (a) monolingual transcribed speech data; (b) monolingual language modelling training data; or (c) parallel corpora of translated text data. This means that separate ASR and MT systems will generally have the benefit of training on much larger datasets.

I think you should know something. You know. I ...										
y	=	0	0	0	0	0	1	0	1	0	$\cdots$
token	=	*i*	*think*	*you*	*should*	*know*	*something*	*you*	*know*	*i*	$\cdots$
x dep	=	*nsubj*	*root*	*nsubj*	*aux*	*ccomp*	*obj*	*nsubj*	*acl : relcl*	*nsubj*	$\cdots$
pos	=	*PRON*	*VERB*	*PRON*	*AUX*	*VERB*	*PRON*	*PRON*	*VERB*	*PRON*	$\cdots$

Figure 1: An excerpt of subtitles (top) and the corresponding segmentation data derived from it (bottom). Punctuation is to mark boundaries $y_i = 1$. Part-of-speech and dependency relations are parsed from each document.

Corpus	BG		LT	
	P	U	P	U
OpenSub.	164,798	41.9	32,603	49.5
ANALYSIS	215	37.3	312	57.2
DEV	238	–	258	–

Table 1: Number of passages (P) in each dataset and average number of utterances per passage (U).

Lang.	Model	F1 ↑	WD ↓
BG	Sub	**56.78**	**33.9***
	Sub+S	56.40	34.4
LT	Sub	44.14	49.2
	Sub+S	**45.94***	**47.0***

Table 2: Intrinsic evaluation of F1 and windowdiff(WD) on ANALYSIS data. +S indicates models with syntactic features. * indicates statistical significance

3. Datasets

3.1. Segmentation Datasets

We obtain BG and LT subtitles from the OpenSubtitles 2018 corpus (Lison and Tiedemann, 2016), which contains monolingual subtitles for 62 languages drawn from movies and television. We sample 10,000 documents for BG and all available documents for LT (1,976 in total). Sentences within a document are concatenated together. Some documents are impractically long and do not match our shorter evaluation data, so we divide each document into 20 equally sized passages (splitting on segment boundaries), roughly matching the average evaluation document size. In addition to speaker turns in subtitles, we treat any of the characters *():-!?.* as segment boundaries. We split the data into a training (75%) and validation set. See Table 1 for corpus statistics.

3.2. Speech Datasets

To perform extrinsic evaluation of a STTT pipeline, we use the speech collections from the MATERIAL[1] program, which aims at finding relevant audio and text documents in low resource languages given English queries. This can be framed as an cross-language information retrieval (CLIR) task, where STTT plays a crucial part in improving the quality of downstream tasks of machine translation and information retrieval.

[1] `www.iarpa.gov/index.php/research-programs/material`

The speech data consists of three domains (news broadcast (NB), topical broadcast (TB) such as podcasts, and conversational speech (CS)) from multiple low-resource languages. NB and TB have one speaker and are more formal, while CS has two and is more casual. For each language, we have two collections of speech documents, the ANALYSIS and DEV sets (each containing a mix of NB, TB, and CS). Only the ANALYSIS datasets include ground truth transcriptions (including segmentation), allowing us to evaluate segmentation and translation quality. However, we can use both datasets for the extrinsic CLIR evaluation since MATERIAL provides English queries with ground truth relevance judgements.

4. Segmentation Model

We treat ASR segmentation as a sequence tagging problem. Let $x_1, \ldots, x_n \in \mathcal{V}^n$ be a passage of n ASR output tokens drawn from a finite vocabulary $\mathcal{V}$. We also define an indicator variable y_i for each token, where $y_i = 1$ indicates a segment boundary between tokens x_i and x_{i+1}. Each token x_i is additionally associated with a corresponding POS tag and dependency label. An example input and output are shown in Figure 1.

We explore a Long Short-Term Memory (LSTM)-based model architecture for this task. In the input layer we represent each word as a 256-dimensional word embedding; when using syntactic information, we also concatenate its POS tag and dependency label embeddings (both 32-dimensional). POS tags and dependency labels are obtained using the UDPipe 2.4 parser (Straka and Straková, 2017). Since we do not have punctuation on actual ASR output, we parse each document with this information removed. Conversational speech between two speakers comes in separate channels for each speaker so we concatenate the output of each channel and treat it as a distinct document when performing segmentation. The segmentation are then merged back into one document using segmentation timestamp information before being used in downstream evaluations.

We then apply a bi-directional LSTM to the input sequence of embeddings to obtain a sequence of n hidden states, each of 256 dimensions (after concatenating the output of each direction). Each output state is then passed through a linear projection layer with logistic sigmoid output to compute the probability of a segment boundary $p(y_i = 1|x)$. The log-likelihood of a single passage/boundary annotation pair is $\log p(y|x) = \sum_{i=1}^{n} \log p(y_i|x)$. All embeddings and parameters are learned by minimizing the negative log-likelihood on the training data using stochastic gradient descent.

Lang.	Model	EDI-NMT			UMD-NMT			UMD-SMT		
		NB	TB	CS	NB	TB	CS	NB	TB	CS
BG	Acous.	24.49	24.65	7.13	**33.25**	29.82	10.32	**35.30**	31.11	11.08
	Sub	24.83	**25.28**	**8.07**	32.89	**30.35**	11.10	35.15	**31.55**	11.32
	Sub+S	**24.90**	25.25	8.04	32.96	30.23	**11.24**	35.16	**31.55**	**11.57**
LT	Acous.	**16.03**	**17.00**	**6.53**	**16.31**	**18.67**	**5.92**	**16.52**	**17.60**	**6.34**
	Sub	14.83	15.59	6.33	15.41	17.47	4.66	15.93	17.14	5.86
	Sub+S	14.97	15.77	6.43	15.40	17.54	5.11	15.76	17.19	6.00

Table 3: Document level BLEU scores on ANALYSIS set. +S indicates model with syntactic features.

Lang.	Model	EDI-NMT			UMD-NMT			UMD-SMT		
		NB	TB	CS	NB	TB	CS	NB	TB	CS
BG	Acous.	0.289	**0.482**	0.052	0.394	0.175	0.005	0.426	0.355	0.148
	Sub	0.289	0.435	**0.127**	0.475	0.19	**0.111**	**0.433**	0.361	**0.245**
	Sub+S	**0.312**	0.443	0.014	**0.498**	**0.247**	0.074	**0.433**	**0.368**	**0.245**
LT	Acous.	0.293	**0.304**	0.005	0.356	0.291	0.0	0.359	**0.484**	0.0
	Sub	0.293	0.266	0.011	**0.393**	0.278	0.0	**0.484**	0.42	0.0
	Sub+S	**0.365**	0.254	**0.111**	0.377	**0.305**	0.0	0.459	0.382	0.0

Table 4: AQWV scores on ANALYSIS set. +S indicates model with syntactic features.

5. Experiments and Results

Pipeline Components All pipeline components were developed by participants in the MATERIAL program (Oard et al., 2019). We use the ASR system developed jointly by the University of Cambridge and the University of Edinburgh (Ragni and Gales, 2018; Carmantini et al., 2019).

We evaluate with three different MT systems. We use the neural MT model developed by the University of Edinburgh (EDI-NMT) (Junczys-Dowmunt et al., 2018) and the neural and phrase-based statistical MT systems from the University of Maryland, UMD-NMT and UMD-SMT respectively (Niu et al., 2018).

For the IR system, we use the bag-of-words query model implemented in Indri (Strohman et al., 2005).

5.1. Intrinsic Evaluation

We evaluate the models on F-measure of the boundary prediction labels, as well as WindowDiff (Pevzner and Hearst, 2002), a metric that penalizes difference in the number of boundaries between the reference and predicted segmentation given a fixed window. We obtain a reference segmentation as described in subsection 3.1. We indicate our models without and with syntactic features as Sub and Sub+S respectively. Table 2 shows our results on the ANALYSIS data. For BG, which is trained on an order of magnitude more data, the model without syntactic information performs slightly better. Meanwhile, in the lower-data LT setting, adding syntactic cues yields a 2.2 point improvement on WindowDiff.

5.2. Extrinsic Evaluations

We perform several extrinsic evaluations using a pipeline of ASR, ASR segmentation, MT, and information retrieval (IR) components.

5.2.1. MT Evaluation

Our first extrinsic evaluation measures the BLEU (Papineni et al., 2002) score of the MT output on the ANALYSIS sets, where we have ground truth reference English translations. As our baseline, we compare the same pipeline using the segmentation produced by the acoustic model of the ASR system, denoted Acous.

Since each segmentation model produces segments with different boundaries, we are unable to use BLEU directly to compare to the reference sen- tences. Thus, we concatenate all segments of a document and treat them as one segment, which we refer to as "document-level" BLEU score. Table 3 shows our results.

For BG, both Sub and Sub+S models improve BLEU scores over the baseline segmentation on the more informal domains (TB, CS). Across all MT systems, Sub+S performs best on conversations (CS), while Sub performs best on topical monologues (TB).

For LT, the segmentation models do not provide any improvement on BLEU scores. However, there is generally an increase in BLEU with the syntactic features, consistent with the intrinsic results.

5.2.2. Document-level CLIR Evaluation

Our second extrinsic evaluation is done on the MATERIAL CLIR task. We are given English queries and asked to retrieve conversations in either BG or LT. In our setup, we only search over the English translations produced by our pipeline. We evaluate the performance of CLIR using the Actual Query Weighted Value (AQWV) (NIST, 2017). Table 4 shows the results of the CLIR ANALYSIS evaluation.

Similar trends are found on the DEV set. On BG, our models yield large increases in AQWV for both UMD MT models, especially on CS, where the gains are on the order of 0.1 absolute points. Syntactic information also proves use-

Lang.	Model	EDI-NMT			UMD-NMT			UMD-SMT		
		NB	TB	SMT	CS	TB	CS	NB1	TB	CS
BG	Acous.	0.583	0.258	0.065	**0.716**	**0.305**	**0.075**	0.725	0.312	**0.139**
	Sub	**0.774**	**0.266**	0.071	0.658	0.296	0.037	**0.675**	0.383	0.076
	Sub+S	**0.774**	0.186	**0.074**	0.658	0.273	0.054	**0.675**	**0.407**	0.105
LT	Acous.	0.161	0.195	0.262	**0.325**	0.307	0.19	**0.372**	**0.404**	0.262
	Sub	**0.348**	0.314	**0.333**	0.271	0.385	**0.262**	0.304	0.386	0.262
	Sub+S	0.269	**0.317**	**0.333**	**0.300**	**0.390**	**0.262**	0.320	0.385	0.262

Table 5: AQWV scores on DEV set. +S indicates model with syntactic features.

Lang.	MT	Relevance	
		A	M
BG	EDI-NMT	0.564	**0.566**
	UMD-NMT	0.572	**0.615**
	UMD-SMT	0.593	**0.658**
	Reference	0.862	
LT	EDI-NMT	**0.576**	0.554
	UMD-NMT	**0.663**	0.593
	UMD-SMT	**0.681**	0.614
	Reference	0.9	

Table 6: Passage-level evaluation comparing relevance using the Sub+S model (M), the acoustic baseline (A).Evaluation of reference translation is also provided for each language.

ful, as Sub+S performs best in six of nine settings. Despite the lack of increase in BLEU for LT, the segmentation models show large increases in AQWV over the baseline, especially on UMD-SMT/NB where the Sub model improves AQWV by 0.125 points absolutely. Only EDI-NMT was able to yield nonzero retrieval scores for the CS domain, with Sub+S improving by 0.106 points.

5.2.3. Passage-level CLIR Evaluation

We also conduct a human evaluation to compare our segmentation model with acoustically-based segmentation and investigate which makes it easier for annotators to determine MT quality and query relevance. To this end, we collect relevant query/passage pairs and ask Amazon Mechanical Turk Workers[2] to judge quality and relevance.

The MT quality judgments were done on a 7-point scale (integer scores from -3 to 3 inclusive), and the query relevance judgments on a 3-point scale (0, 0.5, and 1). A perfect pipeline should achieve 3 in MT quality and 1 in query relevance. We give each HIT (each containing five passages) to three distinct Workers. Figure 2 shows the detailed instruction we have for the HIT. Also see Figure 3 for an example passage as displayed in a HIT.

We require Workers to have a minimum lifetime approval rate of 98% and number of HITs approved greater than 5000. Workers that provide the same quality score for all snippets in a HIT are manual checked by the author.

To generate our evaluation data, we use YAKE! (Campos

et al., 2018) to extract keywords from documents in the ANALYSIS dataset. We then collect 3-segment passages of each document and pair them with a keyword that appears in the middle utterance in the ground truth transcription; these will become the passages and queries we give to Workers. We match the timestamps of these passages in the ground truth transcription with the output of the Sub+S model and the Acous. model, and feed those segments through MT. We randomly sample 200 passages each from BG and LT and present them in three conditions (ground truth or pipeline with either our segmentation, or acoustic segmentation). Please refer to Figure 2 and Figure 3 in the appendix for the instruction and example provided for the Mechanical Turk task.

Table 6 shows the results. We omit the differences in quality because they were not significant. The human reference transcriptions received 0.917 (BG) and 1.153 (LT) out of a maximum of 3.0, suggesting that speech excerpts, even when well translated, are hard to understand out of context. On the relevance assessment, we see consistent improvements in BG using the Sub+S model, regardless of the MT system, although only UMD-SMT is statistically significant.[3]

We do not see improvements on relevance on LT, although no differences are significant. While this might seem counter-intuitive, given that the Sub+S model leads to consistent improvement in LT CLIR, it is corroborated by the lower BLEU scores on LT, suggesting the CLIR pipeline is less affected by poor fluency than are actual human users who need to read the output to determine relevance.

5.3. Discussion

Overall, when subtitle data is plentiful, as is the case with BG, we see consistent improvements on downstream MT and CLIR tasks. Moreover, we find consistent improvements in the CS domain where acoustic segmentation is likely to produce choppy, non-sentence-like segments. Even on LT, where there is not enough data to realize gains in translation, it still has positive effects on the document-level CLIR task.

6. Conclusion

We present an approach for ASR segmentation for low-resource languages for the task of STTT. On extrinsic evaluations of MT, IR, and human evaluations, we are able to

---

[3]Using the approximate randomization test at the $\alpha = .05$ level (Riezler and Maxwell, 2005).

show improvements in the downstream MT and CLIR. In future work, we hope to explore methods to make the tagger model more robust to noise, since word-error rates of ASR in the low-resource condition tend to be high

7. Acknowledgements

This research is based upon work supported inpart by the Office of the Director of National Intelligence (ODNI), Intelligence Advanced Research Projects Activity (IARPA), via contract FA8650-17-C-9117. The views and conclusions contained herein are those of the authors and should not be interpreted as necessarily representing the official policies, either expressed or implied, of ODNI, IARPA, or the U.S. Government. The U.S. Government is authorized to reproduce and distribute reprints for governmental purposes not withstanding any copyright annotation therein.

8. References

Campos, R., Mangaravite, V., Pasquali, A., Jorge, A. M., Nunes, C., and Jatowt, A. (2018). A text feature based automatic keyword extraction method for single documents. In *European Conference on Information Retrieval*, pages 684–691. Springer.

Carmantini, A., Bell, P., and Renals, S. (2019). Untranscribed web audio for low resource speech recognition. In *Proc. Interspeech*.

Cho, E., Niehues, J., and Waibel, A. (2017). Nmt-based segmentation and punctuation insertion for real-time spoken language translation. pages 2645–2649, 08.

Junczys-Dowmunt, M., Grundkiewicz, R., Dwojak, T., Hoang, H., Heafield, K., Neckermann, T., Seide, F., Germann, U., Fikri Aji, A., Bogoychev, N., Martins, A. F. T., and Birch, A. (2018). Marian: Fast neural machine translation in C++. In *Proceedings of ACL 2018, System Demonstrations*, Melbourne, Australia.

Koehn, P. and Knowles, R. (2017). Six challenges for neural machine translation. In *Proceedings of the First Workshop on Neural Machine Translation*, pages 28–39, Vancouver, August. Association for Computational Linguistics.

Lison, P. and Tiedemann, J. (2016). Opensubtitles2016: Extracting large parallel corpora from movie and tv subtitles. In *Proceedings of the Tenth International Conference on Language Resources and Evaluation (LREC 2016)*, pages 923–929.

NIST, (2017). *The Official Original Derivation of AQWV.*

Niu, X., Denkowski, M., and Carpuat, M. (2018). Bidirectional neural machine translation with synthetic parallel data. volume abs/1805.11213, pages 84–91.

Oard, D., Carpuat, M., Galuscakova, P., Barrow, J., Nair, S., Niu, X., Shing, H.-C., Xu, W., Zotkina, E., McKeown, K., Muresan, S., Kayi, E., Eskander, R., Kedzie, C., Virin, Y., Radev, D., Zhang, R., Gales, M., Ragni, A., and Heafield, K. (2019). Surprise languages: Rapid-response cross-language ir. In Nicola Ferro, et al., editors, *Proceedings of the Ninth International Workshop on Evaluating Information Access (EVIA 2019)*, page 23. ACM, 6.

Papineni, K., Roukos, S., Ward, T., and Zhu, W.-J. (2002). Bleu: a method for automatic evaluation of machine translation. In *Proceedings of the 40th annual meeting on association for computational linguistics*, pages 311–318. Association for Computational Linguistics.

Pevzner, L. and Hearst, M. A. (2002). A critique and improvement of an evaluation metric for text segmentation. *Computational Linguistics*, 28(1):19–36.

Pham, N.-Q., Nguyen, T.-S., Ha, T.-L., Hussain, J., Schneider, F., Niehues, J., Stüker, S., and Waibel, A. (2019). The iwslt 2019 kit speech translation system.

Ragni, A. and Gales, M. (2018). Automatic speech recognition system development in the "wild". In *Proc. Interspeech*.

Riezler, S. and Maxwell, J. T. (2005). On some pitfalls in automatic evaluation and significance testing for MT. In *Proceedings of the ACL Workshop on Intrinsic and Extrinsic Evaluation Measures for Machine Translation and/or Summarization*, pages 57–64, Ann Arbor, Michigan, June. Association for Computational Linguistics.

Sperber, M., Pham, N. Q., Nguyen, T. S., Niehues, J., Müller, M., Ha, T.-L., Stüker, S., and Waibel, A. (2018). Kit's iwslt 2018 slt translation system.

Sridhar, V. K. R., Chen, J., Bangalore, S., Ljolje, A., and Chengalvarayan, R. (2013). Segmentation strategies for streaming speech translation. In *HLT-NAACL*.

Straka, M. and Straková, J. (2017). Tokenizing, pos tagging, lemmatizing and parsing ud 2.0 with udpipe. In *Proceedings of the CoNLL 2017 Shared Task: Multilingual Parsing from Raw Text to Universal Dependencies*, pages 88–99, Vancouver, Canada, August. Association for Computational Linguistics.

Strohman, T., Metzler, D., Turtle, H., and Croft, W. B. (2005). Indri: A language model-based search engine for complex queries. In *Proceedings of the International Conference on Intelligent Analysis*, volume 2, pages 2–6. Citeseer.

Vila, L. C., Escolano, C., Fonollosa, J. A. R., and Costa-jussà, M. R. (2018). End-to-end speech translation with the transformer. In *IberSPEECH*.

A. Additional Document-level CLIR Evaluation

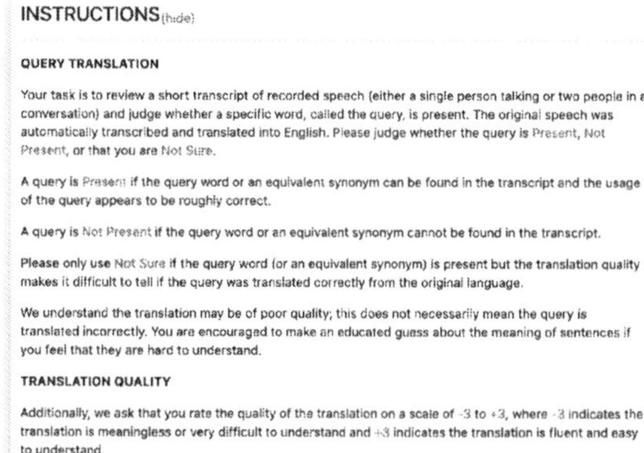

Figure 2: The instructions we provided for the Mechanical Turk task.

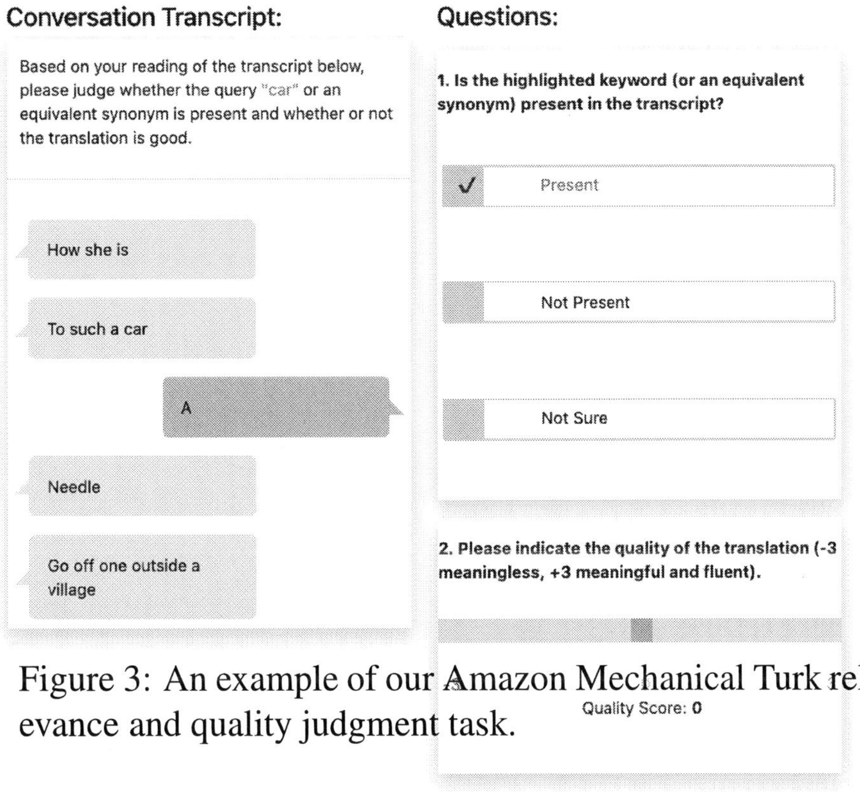

Figure 3: An example of our Amazon Mechanical Turk relevance and quality judgment task.